TO:

FROM:
Brother Craig

Pop Smoke
The Memoir of a 1ˢᵗ Cavalry Division Grunt
Vietnam/Cambodia 1969-1970

By Sgt. Ralph Dagenhart

July 2024

Copyright © 2022 by A15 Publishing

All rights reserved. Published by A15 Publishing.

No part of this publication may be reproduced, distributed, or transmitted in any form or by any means, including photocopying, recording, or other electronic or mechanical methods, without the prior written permission of the publisher, except in the case of brief quotations embodied in critical reviews and certain other noncommercial uses permitted by copyright law. For permission requests, write to the publisher, addressed "Attention: Permissions Coordinator," at the address below or by e-mail at info@a15publishing.com

The views expressed in this publication are those of the author and do not necessarily reflect the official policy or position of the Department of Defense or the U.S. Government.

A15 Publishing
5219 Monticello Avenue #5037
Williamsburg, VA 23188-9998
www.A15publishing.com

ISBN 978-1-970155-22-8

FIRST PRINTING

Dedication

To Richard and Phillip, my sons; to Kaitlyn, Carson, Dylan, and Taylor, my grandchildren; this memoir is written to you. My military service is a part of my life that you know little about because I haven't spoken much to you concerning it. For combat veterans, especially infantry soldiers, this is not uncommon. There are many things we've experienced in war that we would wish to forget, but that is not possible. But my experience is not unique to other combat infantry veterans. We all faced the same fears, the same emotional upheavals from injuries and deaths, and the same survival guilt regardless of the war or conflict involved.

My hope, as you read this, is that you will come to understand what a significant impact this experience had on me and how its effect has made a difference in the way I approach life. My opinions and attitudes today, not just about my life, but also about our great country and the faith I have for my Creator, reflect a lot on that challenging time in military service so long ago.

Ralph Dagenhart

Murphy's Laws of Combat Operations

1. Friendly Fire – isn't.
2. If at first you don't succeed, call in an airstrike.
3. Never share a foxhole with anyone braver than yourself.
4. Never draw fire: it irritates everyone around you.
5. Never forget that your weapon was made by the lowest bidder.
6. The enemy invariably attacks on two occasions: when they're ready, and when you're not.
7. There is no such thing as a perfect plan.
8. Five second fuses always burn three seconds.
9. Teamwork is essential; it gives the enemy other people to shoot at.
10. If the enemy is in range, so are you.
11. Radios will fail as soon as you need fire support.
12. Anything you do can get you killed, including nothing.
13. Tracers work both ways.
14. Military intelligence is a contradiction.
15. The one item you need is always in short supply.
16. It's not the one with your name on it; it's the one addressed "to whom it may concern" you've got to be worried about.
17. If your Platoon Sergeant can see you, so can the enemy.
18. When in doubt, empty your magazine.
19. Whenever you have plenty of ammo you never miss. If low on ammo, you can't hit the broad side of a barn.
20. Field experience is something you don't get until just after you need it.

Pop Smoke

The command given to detonate a smoke grenade. The smoke emitted was used to mark a unit's position under assault to alert aerial support from firing on friendlies. The smoke also gave the helicopter pilots the direction of the wind, a critical fact needed in flying their aircraft. In addition, a smoke grenade was used to mark a unit's position for an incoming helicopter bringing supplies, etc.... The pilot had to recognize and report the color of the smoke to the ground forces to be sure it was from friendlies.

"Pop Smoke" is a true account of an infantry soldier's one year combat experience in a strange country known as South Vietnam in 1969-70. The gunfire, the explosions, the bloodshed, and the deaths, were no different from that faced by grunts of other wars and conflicts. The day-to-day existence under Mother Nature's elements was the same as those who lived in foxholes and slept under the stars before him. The infantry mission was very simple; locate, attack, and destroy the enemy. In doing so, grunts depended upon each other in order to survive. This too, has not changed. The thing that is different; the civilian leadership did not have the will to win the war. The military was prevented from doing what was needed to win a victory. As a result, billions of dollars were spent by the United States executing this war; over fifty-eight thousand Americans lost their lives fighting in the war, thousands more suffered wounds from this conflict, and the South Vietnamese people are living under a Communist regime today.

Introduction

*Of all the medals upon our chests
From battles and wars we knew
The one admired as the very best
Is the one of infantry blue*

*It's only a rifle upon a wreath
So why should it mean so much?
It is what it took to earn it
That gives it that Touch.*

*To earn this special accolade
You faced the enemy's fire
Whether you survived or not
God dialed that one desire.*

*For those of us who served the cause
And brought this nation glory
It's the Combat Infantryman's Badge
That really tells the story.*

September 12, 1946 was the day that I came into this world, making my parents very happy. They had been married for ten years trying to produce children, but to no avail. My mom became pregnant early in marriage, but lost this baby during pregnancy. My dad was drafted into the army in December 1942, thus separated from mom most of the time during the war. He was discharged from army duty in November 1945, and I was born the next year. I would be the only baby born to this union.

My parents were typical of most other parents in the small town of Troutman, North Carolina. They lived very conservative lifestyles with very little money to spend beyond the essentials. We lived in a small, four room frame house with one bath on a one-third acre lot that my parents were able to purchase after a few years of marriage. My mom worked in the local cotton mill until it closed in 1962, but she still remained in textiles. My dad was a furniture worker most of his life. Neither one finished high school and they were pleased with my graduation in 1964, but disappointed when I chose my senior year not to enroll in a college. I would say we were considered to be in the lower end of middle class. They were the WWII generation and never bought anything with borrowed money. If they wanted to purchase something and did not have the money, they saved the amount needed before they bought the article. My mom and dad were Christians who attended church regularly, made sure I was there also, and taught me about right and wrong and how to live life successfully. My dad passed away at 91 years of age; mom was 96 years old when she died. I could not have asked for better parents; they were the best.

Since both parents were employed, I began my childhood during the day under the responsibility of one of my mom's sisters. My aunt had a daughter and a son. Sam was just ten months older than me and we were together all the time as playmates. He became the brother I never had. Usually, when trouble happened, it most always involved both of us. I tried to convince myself that he, being the oldest, was the one who caused us to get into trouble in the first place. The house that they lived in had no underpinning. It was high enough off the ground that as kids we could play under most of it. Sam and I received brand new pedal cars one Christmas when we were probably four years old.

Me in Pedal Car with Pet

We were under the house with our new cars one day when my aunt heard us beating on something. She asked us what we were doing and our response was "nothing". With that answer she suspected something, so she came from the house and found us doing body work on our new pedal cars. We both got our behinds warmed for trying to destroy our cars. Our parents sacrificed much to be able to purchase them for us.

    I don't remember, but I have been told that Sam and I would play outside in the summertime with just our underpants on. At times we would take them off and the neighbors passing by would get a laugh at us running around without clothes. Evidently, we had no problem with nudity outside, but we were also told that when bath time came, we didn't want anyone in the room. I don't remember any of this, but I stick by my story.

    Another incident I have no recollection of involved a bathroom visit, only it wasn't a bathroom. My aunt and uncle did not have a bathroom in their house. Like a lot of country folk, they had an outhouse instead. I was using this facility one day and started hollering loudly. My aunt was in the middle of baking bread when she heard my screams and was terrified that I had fallen through the hole. She ran as fast as she could and found that I had just dropped my underpants into the hole instead. Naturally, she was greatly relieved.

    When I started school, my grandmother came to live with us after my dad added two additional rooms onto our house to accommodate her. So she became the one to get me to the bus in the morning and to welcome me home in the afternoon. She functioned as a second mom and at her death in 1977, I felt as though I had lost my mom. Sam and I would not be together as much but we were usually in the same class at school for the first five years. He still acted as a big brother, always protecting me from bigger guys who wanted to bully me. I was one of the smallest boys in our class and he made sure that a bigger guy did not pick on me. As we entered adulthood, we continued to see each other regularly. Sam was drafted into the army and was sent to South Vietnam several years before me. He was the one I called to pick me up at the Charlotte airport the day I came from my Vietnam tour. I wanted to surprise my wife and parents because they didn't know exactly when I would get home once back in the states. Like a big brother, Sam dropped everything he was doing and immediately came to the airport. After his military service, he had a business running a service station and doing minor car repair work. So I usually bought fuel from him and he serviced my cars on a regular basis. Some years ago, he moved to the far end of the state and I don't get to see him very often. I think we both miss that brotherly relationship we had for so long.

During my childhood, baseball was the nation's game. Like other boys in the community, I loved this game and began playing organized baseball in Little League. I spent many hours in the back yard pretending I was at the plate with a 3-2 count looking to hit the next pitch from Bob Gibson over the fence and win the game. The Yankees were my professional team. They had Yogi Berra, Mickey Mantle, Roger Maris, Whitey Ford, and a second baseman, Bobby Richardson, who I tried to emulate. I continued to advance to the various age groups and made the high school team starting at second base my junior and senior years. I never became the great batter I envisioned in my younger years, but I did become a pretty good fielder and did not commit many errors. After graduation, I played softball until my mid-thirties, still enjoying the game. But family responsibilities took priority, and time to play ball became less and less.

Second Baseman

I look back at this time when things were not so fast-paced; people's word and a handshake meant something; and drugs were medicine prescribed by a doctor. We could hardly wait to get our drivers licenses; it meant more freedom. And to get that first car, it didn't matter if it was not new. I loved those 50s and 60s models and continue to be an old car enthusiast to this day. My first car was a

1958 Ford and I presently own a 1965 model that I bought new after finishing high school. Cruising in town on Friday and Saturday nights with our special friends was a must back then. Hanging out at curbside restaurants on the weekends was also the norm. They had names like: J C's Toot 'n' Tellum, Miller's BBQ, Rotonda, Scottie's, and Tastee Freeze. For spending money, I worked part time at a local Amoco service station during my high school years. I enjoyed pumping gas, servicing vehicles, and washing cars and trucks. It was good training for any young person, but the pay was not very promising. Still, it taught me a lot about the everyday work ethic expected of us all.

With Future Wife at Our Prom

In the fall of 1960, I began the school year as a freshman in high school. Good ole "rock and roll" was beginning to make an impact with artists like the Big Bopper, Buddy Holly, and Elvis Presley. The economy in our country was doing very well. Our parents, who won World War II, were providing the means for us to have a better life than they had growing up. As teenagers, we were having a good time and those four years in high school bring back fond memories. I'll never forget the senior trip to Washington, D.C. and New York City. That was the year for the world's fair and seeing the displays from other countries of the globe was very educational. This was also the first time the public was given the opportunity to see the new Ford Mustang. What a success story this car has been over the years! Our country was enjoying a relatively peaceful time, although the "cold war" with Russia and China had been going on since the end of WWII. The exceptions were the insertion of American troops into Lebanon in 1955 and the 1962 showdown with Russia over the deployment of missiles in Cuba.

Halfway around the world was a country most Americans had never heard of in the early part of the decade. By the end of the 60s, it was almost impossible not to know about South Vietnam. Until recent years, the war that the United States fought there would be the longest in U.S. history. It would cause almost 3 million American military men and women to serve there, with 6 million more supporting them around the world. When the guns fell silent, almost 2 million soldiers, representing several countries, lost their lives to this war.

South Vietnam was a small country about the size of Washington State, containing 44 provinces with a population of almost 16 million people at the beginning of 1960. It was 585 miles long and 100 miles wide, located in a part of the world known as Southeast Asia. Three quarters of the population were engaged in agriculture, growing rice, tea, and coffee. Harvesting the sap from rubber trees was also a part of their farming.

Prior to WWII, Southeast Asia was a part of the French Empire and known as French Indochina. Seeking world domination, the Japanese invaded this area, including China, early in WWII. Three years after the Japanese were defeated, South Vietnam continued to be a part of the French Empire, but was allowed to become a constitutional monarchy. The communists in the North, led by Ho Chi Minh, began in 1946 to take control of this area away from the French. This became known as the Indo-China War and culminated in a French defeat in 1954. The country was separated at the 17th parallel with North Vietnam organizing a communist government and South Vietnam with a resemblance of a democracy. The United States had been giving aid to the area starting in 1950. With the communist threat from the North increasing, military advisors were sent to South Vietnam in 1956 to begin training the South Vietnamese. By the time the United States sent ground forces into the South in the summer of 1965, the war had escalated considerably.

This was a strange country with a language unknown to me that I spent one year of my life trying to survive and make some sense of. By the time I arrived in the country in the summer of 1969, our military had been heavily involved for four years. Until the beginning of 1968, a majority of the people of our country were supporting the war. After the big Tet Offensive of that year, the support went away. When I came home in June, 1970, the anti-war movement was at its peak, the people were tired of war, and those of us who fought in it were looked upon as dangerous "baby killers."

Naturally, I have some strong opinions of this war that I know something about. First, I believe our national intentions were right in executing this war. Remembering the history of that time reminds us that Russia and China were superpowers who were trying to inject communist influence and power around the world. South Vietnam, along with Southeast Asia, was a major goal in their plans. We, on the other hand, were trying to stop them from enslaving countries with their doctrine of servitude to the communist state. The Russians had already taken a number of eastern European nations such as Hungary and Poland under their influence and domination. Second, when sending young men and women into battle, the goal is to win with a strategy and a plan that will achieve this. Our political leaders didn't have the will to allow the military to do what was needed to win. We didn't lose the war as some have said; cowardly politicians wouldn't allow us to win it. If the conditions to win are not in place, we should never sacrifice the lives of our young people in a war we choose not to win. Third, no other generation of men and women who serve our country in uniform should be treated like 2nd class citizens as Vietnam veterans have been. In transitioning back to civilian life after my tour, I realized no one but family and close friends really cared about my military service. Therefore, most of us Vietnam veterans didn't wear anything that would indicate we had served. We also did not record this on a resume because some companies would not hire anyone who served in Vietnam. In recent years, we have gotten a lot of thanks for our service, but it has been a long time in coming. In saying this, I don't mean to sound as if I'm bitter; I'm not. Some Vietnam veterans still remain this way, but I hope they can finally confront their bitterness and resolve it. Fourth, the news media was allowed too much access to ground operations. The daily video of people injured and killed was something the American public did not need to see. Also, the media put their spin on the war's progress, usually trying to make the case that we were losing.

This actually was the way they portrayed the big Tet offensive of 1968. The commander of all North Vietnamese forces, General Vo

Nguyen Giap, admitted in his memoir several years later, that their military was finished after their offensive. Quoting from his words, he said: "What we still don't understand is why you Americans stopped the bombing of Hanoi. You had us on the ropes. If you had pressed us a little harder just for another day or two, we were ready to surrender! It was the same at the battle of Tet. You defeated us! We knew it, and we thought you knew it. But we were elated to notice your media was helping us. They were causing more disruption in America than we could in the battlefields. We were ready to surrender. You had won!

There is a quote from an unknown author about the media. It states: "Do not fear the enemy, for they can take only your life... fear the media, for they will destroy your honor." How true this has been for the Vietnam veteran.

This was a war of America's choosing. I was a part of the fighting force that our leaders chose to send to this country that was being invaded by a well-trained, well-disciplined, enemy force. The nation called. I reported for duty. This is my story.

The American infantryman or grunt is truly a noble creature. For alone among all of the others in the military, his mission is the most dangerous; to close with and destroy the enemy by close personal combat. He stands with his rifle and courage at the very tip of the military spear.

LTC John Hedley, USA, Retired
Recon Platoon Leader, Vietnam, author of **"Saddle Up"**
The Story of a Red Scarf

As I write this, almost five decades have passed since my tour of duty as an infantryman ended in Vietnam. Yet, even with these passing years, some memories of that time are still very vivid in my mind. Where the years have clouded or erased recollections of events or persons, I have been assisted in recapturing those memories of long ago. Several guys in my battalion got together at a reunion in Detroit in 1992 and formed the 5th Battalion, 7th Cavalry Association. When I became aware of this, I began attending the reunions. It was at one of these that I obtained a copy of my unit's weekly action reports. These reports have helped to put the events into the proper time frame of my tour. Declassified material from the 1st Cavalry Division has become available in recent years to add to this memoir. I've also been fortunate to reunite at the reunions with some of my buddies with whom I served. They have shared their memories of the same events. LTC Patrick Dockery, USAR, Retired, has written a memoir about his tour with the battalion as a company commander and supply officer during the same time that I was there. "Vietnam Was More Than Just The Killing" is a very descriptive account of the day-to-day life of an infantry unit and personnel. His book has reminded me of the times we were able to relax and get away from patrolling and combat for just a few hours or a few days. This kept us sane.

    In this, my memoir, I have recorded the events with the knowledge that some of the facts may still be unknown, thus giving an incomplete picture of what truly happened. However, for reasons given above, I believe my account to be as accurate a description as possible in a far-away land where death and destruction came to be expected. I have also tried to describe my thoughts, feelings, and attitudes that played a part in my actions then and are still influencing my life today.

XIV

Chapter 1:
Duty, Honor, Country

The most precious commodity with which the Army deals in is the individual soldier who is the heart and soul of our combat forces.
-General J. Lawton Collins
War II Senior Officer

January 27th, 1969 is one of those dates for me that is not easily forgotten. After a three-year job deferment ended in November, 1968, I received one of those form letters from Uncle Sam that millions of other young men received. It changed my status from civilian worker to government employee. The letter came in the mail just before Christmas, with orders to report to the Statesville bus station for transfer to the Charlotte induction center on that unforgettable day in 1969.

In the summer of 1965, classified as 1-A (eligible for the draft), I had decided to join the Air Force to avoid being drafted. My employer had tried to persuade me to participate in a North Carolina Department of Labor apprenticeship program that would exempt being drafted for three years. I was looking for a better job, but the war prevented most companies from hiring young men who stood the chance of being drafted. I took the required testing and received a date to report to Lackland Air Force base for basic training. A buddy and friend, Hal, had convinced me to choose the Air Force. He had enlisted and we were headed to Texas together. However, my father had received a report from a recent medical exam with the doctor suspecting he may have tuberculosis. Without knowing the length of time my dad would be staying in the hospital, I chose to accept the three-year job deferment. I believe my friend has forgiven me for not joining him in the Air Force. After a short period of time, my dad was released from the hospital with no sign of the disease. When the deferment ended three years later, I was re-classified 1-A and expected to be drafted. I married my fiancée in 1967, so the decision to volunteer again was not a priority. I decided to take a chance with the draft. Even though I believe the Air Force would have been a less dangerous commitment, I do not regret the path my service took me. It was a very challenging part of my life and I believe I am a better person because of it. I learned a great deal about myself in a land far away and a culture much different from my own.

There must have been at least fifty of us at the bus station, saying our last goodbyes. I only knew two young men, one of whom lived in the same neighborhood while I was growing up. The other one I knew as a school friend. Most of the day was spent at the induction center checking us physically and mentally to determine our qualifications for military service. Only three or four were disqualified; my friend from childhood being one. He was given the hearing test four times, suspecting he was trying to fool them. Tommy was very worried about military service because his cousin had been killed in Vietnam just a month before our date for induction. He was so relieved to be returning home and I was happy for him. Our last duty before leaving the induction center was to raise our right hands and swear to defend our country and its constitution. I was officially a member of the United States military.

After supper, we boarded buses to travel to Fort Bragg, North Carolina. This would be our home for the next nine weeks, where we would learn what soldiering was all about. Only three hours from home, I hoped that I would get to come home at least once during training. I did get home twice, but without permission. Had I been caught, I would have been punished for being AWOL (absent without leave). The significance of Fort Bragg to our family did not immediately come to mind at that time. However, my dad would later remind me that he had been there exactly twenty-five years earlier prior to his overseas deployment to Europe in World War II. He landed on Utah beach, Normandy, France, the July day, 1944, when the Allies broke out of the beachhead and began the long struggle to eventually invade Germany itself and end the war in Europe. Participating in this struggle, my dad would earn four medals and fight in four major battles. One of those was the Battle of the Bulge that was fought during the coldest European winter in fifty years.

We arrived at the reception station on Fort Bragg late in the night. Because of the hour, we were given bedrolls and assigned billets. Early the next morning, we were rudely awakened by a corporal (lowest rank NCO) and marched to the mess hall for breakfast. The rest of the day and week was spent processing the records needed for military service, drawing uniforms, learning to march like a soldier, and of course, getting the G.I. haircut. By the end of the week, we had also received numerous shots, had been tested for skills and aptitude, and had learned some military procedures.

Finally, late on Friday of this first week, we were trucked to our training area and met our new "dad", our drill sergeant. Our official training would begin the following week and the Staff Sergeant would be with us constantly day and night during most of our eight weeks of basic training. It would be his job to guide, instruct, and encourage us during training. Staff Sergeant Ross was a graduate of drill sergeants' school; a course which reviews all the "basics" of basic training in a curriculum much more strenuous than basic training itself. But he also had the experience; he was a combat infantry veteran of the Vietnam War. He wore the CIB (Combat Infantry Badge) on his chest. I would also proudly wear the CIB later as an infantry combat veteran. This award means more to me than any other decoration I received for my service. Many soldiers desire to wear the CIB, but this award is for the few who meet the requirements.

First, the soldier's MOS (Military Occupational Specialty) must be infantry. Second, an infantry soldier must be assigned to an infantry unit. Third, in this assignment, a soldier must be in a hostile environment and satisfactorily perform his duty in active combat against enemy forces. Just being in a war zone will not count for this award. No amount of documented time in actual combat has been specified to receive this award.

S.Sgt. Ross knew better than we did the things we would need to learn to prepare us for future combat. I remember him as a very disciplined, extremely motivated, career soldier whom I admired for his stern, but fair treatment of us as we made the transformation from civilian to soldier. With so many being trained at that time, I'm sure S.Sgt. Ross would not remember me, but I would feel honored to be able to meet him again.

Every United States Army soldier begins his military service learning the basics of infantry tactics and skills for use in combat. Regardless of the soldier's eventual MOS, he is trained to fight as an infantry rifleman, if the need arises. There have been instances in combat where cooks, clerks, and other support personnel have had to revert to their infantry training to fight off an enemy unit. Basic infantry training is one of the toughest things a person can do. It tests a person's character and forces a soldier to do things he did not expect he could do. The eight-week training cycle consisted of 352 hours of instruction, practice, practical exercise, and testing on 29 subjects. This extensive program was designed to transform a trainee into a proficient military athlete, an expert marksman, and most importantly, a self- reliant, mature soldier, who is able to act, not only on orders of others, but also on his own initiative. This is one clear advantage that the United States military has that other militaries in some countries do not have.

Everyone expected to be harassed during basic training. We had read about this and had family members who had served in the military. They had passed this information along to us. Most of us had not had any previous military training so mistakes, foul-ups, and stupid errors were bound to bring harassment on most of us. We learned to accept the humiliation knowing this was one way the military prepares its soldiers for the stress of combat. But harassment in combat is another matter. In my opinion, there is no excuse for it. Most veterans have a low tolerance for someone who uses his rank or position to abuse an individual or combat unit in this way. Sometimes in Vietnam we didn't know who was doing the harassing. On a number of occasions, we would already be in our NDP (Night Defensive Position) when word would come down to move to another location to avoid a B-52 strike. We could be no closer than three kilometers, but the ground still shook and the noise from the explosions were very loud even at that distance. It was my belief that battalion HQ knew early enough about the strike to warn us before setting up for the night. I have since learned from a B-52 pilot that this was not the case.

However, because of the late warning, many times we found ourselves setting up in our NDP after sunset. This was not good. It put us in a very weak defensive posture. We needed daylight to set up for maximum security and defense.

Another incident in training comes to mind. Early on we were told that the company that attained the highest scores in marksmanship would receive a weekend pass. Qualifying on the rifle range was one of the things I enjoyed most because of my early life hunting rabbits and squirrels. I was already accustomed to firearms. However, the Army wants to train a soldier its way to eliminate any bad habits with a rifle that the soldier might have. I was very disappointed in my score for the M-14. I realized at the end of qualifying that my front sight had been bumped and misaligned during lunch break. I suspected someone grabbed my rifle after lunch, then realized he had the wrong one and bumped the sight when he put it back in the rifle rack. I know that I would have scored much higher if I had noticed the problem. I was hitting the targets very well during the morning qualification. I did qualify later as an Expert with the M-16 and M-60 machine gun. The companies, as a unit, did attain the highest scores in the battalion, but I did not see anyone from my company receive a pass for the weekend. That really angered me and that's the reason I risked coming home on two weekends without a pass. It was foolish to do and I would have been punished if caught, but I let my selfish desire overrule the discipline that the Army was trying to teach me. That would be important to remember in combat. Without discipline, lives can be lost unnecessarily, and combat missions can fail with horrifying results.

As winter turned to spring, approximately 175 trainees from A Company, 9th Battalion, 2nd Training Brigade, officially became Army soldiers on graduation day, March 28, 1969. The next day we would learn the additional training each of us would receive. This would determine our military job as long as we served. I don't recall sleeping much that night, trying to anticipate where my training would take me next. I didn't have long to wait; the next morning we were called to formation and given our orders. I was promoted to E-2, which paid a few more dollars a month. My assignment sent me to Fort Dix, New Jersey, for additional infantry training. There would be no leave at this time, and I would be on a bus heading north before lunch. With these orders I was positive I would be spending time in Korea or Vietnam when this training was completed. The odds pointed to South Vietnam. Basic training was tough, but I had no problems with it. I did well with each aspect of the training and I'm sure this was the reason for the promotion in rank. Just a small number of us were promoted at the completion of basic training. Most of the others were also headed for additional infantry training but a few received orders to train for different jobs in the army. I remember one young man who was returned to his civilian job at the Pentagon without any further training. Someone he knew must have wanted him to return. Sometimes, it depends on who you know. However, his pay would be greatly reduced as a private in the military working the same job.

With my Father at Fort Bragg

Graduation Day With a Buddy From a Nearby Town

    I had tried to digest and learn all that had been taught those eight weeks. Now that I knew the job I would be doing for the next 18 months, the importance of additional training took on significant emphasis in my Army life. The nine weeks of advanced infantry training would help to sharpen my skills and teach me to react to combat situations automatically. I knew that going to war was serious business, and my life and the lives of others would depend on my ability to master as much additional training as possible. The training at Fort Dix was more of the same that I had learned in basic but much more intense and involved. I was finally able to get a weekend pass, but had nowhere I wanted to go. A school friend was also in training there and had a brother in the Air Force who was the recruiter in a nearby town. We received passes together for two weekends and were able to sleep at his brother's house at night while we checked out the town. The first weekend we returned to base, we failed to sign in. No one had told us before our departure about this procedure, so we had to report to the commanding officer the next day. We were expecting punishment but after explaining the situation and convincing him that we had returned to base before the 6:00 PM requirement, he did not give us an Article 15, which would have been the punishment for this first offense.

    I did get the opportunity for one more weekend pass. However, the pass was not given because my squad leader failed to get it scheduled. I didn't realize this until my wife and parents showed up on Friday afternoon to spend the weekend with me. My platoon sergeant was very understanding and allowed me to leave stating that he would take care of this for me. My squad leader was in his last training with troops before his tour began in Vietnam. I hope he took better care of those he would lead in combat.

And so, at the end of May, just before Memorial Day, I graduated again from tough training in preparation for jungle warfare. That spring of 1969, I was in the best physical shape ever. I truly thought my training was the best of any army in the world and believed I was ready for combat. But doubts began almost immediately. Would I measure up? Would I let my buddies down? When the lead began to fly for real, would I react as trained? Would I be able to take life as is inevitable with infantry soldiers? Could I live with myself when this happens? Without the experience of combat, no one knows for sure how he will react as trained. I saw several during my tour that could not handle the hostile actions that resulted in death or injury. These soldiers were given other jobs to do, mostly in a support role. A soldier who could not function in a combat infantry environment was detrimental to the unit and could cause lives to be lost unnecessarily. Daily, we depended on each other to survive. With more exposure to hostile fire, the mission became less and less important and keeping everybody alive became the central focus for us grunts.

This was it in a nutshell. We had answered our nation's call and were sent to help a small country threatened by communist invaders. We participated in many missions never once refusing to go into battle. We hoped that our efforts would make a difference. But staying alive and returning home became primary. I suspect this is true of every grunt in all wars and conflicts.

Chapter 2:
Assignment-Republic of Vietnam

I will not escalate or widen the war by bombing the North or by sending American boys to do what Asian boys ought to be doing to protect themselves.
Lyndon B. Johnson
36th President of the United States

Someone evidently forgot to remind President Johnson about his statement that Asian boys should be doing the fighting. By the time I arrived in Vietnam, American boys had been fighting for four years and American advisors had been there for several years prior to that. My reporting date was June 23, 1969, for my one-year tour of duty. I arrived at the overseas assignment center in Oakland, California, the day before to be processed with orders to the 1st Cavalry Division (Air Mobile) in Long Binh, South Vietnam. But before that time arrived, I would spend my first official leave of twenty days at home with my family. I also had some time with my best civilian buddy, Sonny, whose marriage began in the middle of my basic training period. The last few days before my departure were spent with my wife of two years on a trip to the North Carolina mountains and Tennessee. I remember this time as one of joy and sadness. I did not want to leave my wife and family, I was not very excited about my new duty station, but I felt I was no better than anyone else. Others were serving our country, why should I be excluded? Besides, my dad had gone to war and had returned. He was my hero and I respected him very much. It was now my duty; the nation had called. I would go and I firmly believed I would return alive. However, after the first few months, I began to wonder if I would return whole. Little did I know, as anyone who has not been in combat, that when I did return one year later, I was not the same person that left my wife and family. Vietnam would forever change me as it did all others who would serve there.

Days Before Leaving for Vietnam

Free ticket to Southeast Asia

After spending twelve hours at the Oakland center, which was securely locked (no one could leave until a flight was ready), I boarded a commercial airliner for the fourteen-hour trip to my new duty station. South Vietnam is halfway around the globe and required a fuel stop in the Philippines or Guam. We arrived in the early morning hours of June 24th. My first day of my tour was already made before my arrival. My first memory of this country was the immediate temperature at 3:00 A.M. It was extremely warm, and it would be several hours before the sun would rise. I also cannot forget the smell that permeated my nose at that early hour. It was a combination of raw sewage, dead fish and spoiled food. I also remember the thirty-minute bus ride from the Bien Hoa airport to the replacement center in Long Binh. The bus was just like a school bus, but had chicken wire over the outside of the windows. Someone asked the driver about this wire. We were told that this prevented someone from throwing a grenade into the bus. WELCOME TO VIETNAM!

Due to the early hour, no processing could be done until after breakfast. An interesting thing happened after breakfast. I needed to go to the latrine (bathroom) and very quickly found one. As I entered the doorway, I noticed some individuals to the right of me. The latrines had no enclosures for privacy, so they were completely open throughout the facility. I looked to my right and saw about a dozen young South Vietnamese women in the shower area. Although they were not showering, they surprised me by not having their tops and bras on. This embarrassed me and I walked out without using the latrine. I believe they were washing their tops, but I didn't stay long enough to be sure. I learned later that I could have used the latrine and they would have paid me no attention. However, I thought, WHAT A WAY TO START A TOUR!

In Country Training

I reported to the 1st Cavalry Division 1st team academy, located in Long Binh. It was a five-day school designed to orient new personnel on the division's air-mobile procedures used in combat. Classroom training was also given to inform us of the customs and procedures to be used in cooperating with the South Vietnamese military and people. We had to repel from a 32-foot tower to simulate rappelling from a helicopter. I was issued an M-16 rifle, taking time to zero this weapon on the firing range. At the end of this training, I was flown by fixed wing aircraft to LZ Buttons approximately 75 miles northeast of Saigon. LZ Buttons was a large Army base at the foot of a mountain called Nui Ba Ra. This base's airstrip was long enough to accommodate C-130s. A large number of support units were located here, and it was much like an Army base in the states, with amenities available to the troops stationed there. The Vietnamese village of Song Be was near the base and many people from this village worked for the military there.

I was assigned to A company, 5th Battalion, 7th Cavalry. My battalion headquarters was located on LZ Buttons at the time, but all the companies were patrolling in the jungle around the camp. I wouldn't get to enjoy the benefits of this base, because I would have to join my company the next day. During the night, someone came to the tent where I was sleeping and warned a first sergeant sleeping there also that the base was receiving incoming mortars. Since none had fallen inside the perimeter, the top sergeant did not think it important to go to the bunker. He was not too concerned, so I didn't have any trouble going back to sleep.

FSB Buttons in front of the Nui Ba Ra Mountains

I boarded a helicopter the next morning to join my company located north of Buttons near the Cambodian border. This would be my first flight on a Huey helicopter, more commonly known as a "slick." This was the true infantry workhorse in Vietnam. Hueys carried us into battle and picked us up after the battle. They brought us our food, our water, our mail, and all our materials to wage war. Some of the most dangerous missions for them was inserting us into the jungle for a combat assault and picking up our wounded during a battle. They were our heroes. If they didn't come for us, we would not have survived. During the war, over 4,000 pilots and crew members gave their all for us and our country. I still have a special place in my heart for these guys fifty years later. Most of them were in their early twenties and appeared to have no fear. In my one-year tour, I would fly many times with these young warriors and received an air medal for participating in 25 or more combat assaults. As someone has said: this was a helicopter war. There is a lot of truth in this statement. Without this formidable aircraft to transport infantry in a timely manner, we would have been at a great disadvantage.

Combat Assault

Log Bird Re-Supply

Chapter 3:
Historic 1st Cavalry Division (1st Team)

*You cannot choose your battlefield, God does that for you:
but you can plant a standard where a standard never flew.*
-Stephen Crane, *The Colors*

    This statement clearly describes the First Cavalry Division. It was formally activated on September 13, 1921, at Fort Bliss, Texas. Upon activation, the 7th, 8th and 10th Cavalry regiments were assigned with the 1st regiment assigned less than one month earlier. More than a year later, the 5th regiment replaced the 10th and later the 12th replaced the 1st. In the early years, the division patrolled the Mexican border using mostly horses to halt the band of smugglers operating along the border.
    By 1940, the automobile, tank, and aircraft had taken the place of the horse. By 1943, the division processed for overseas deployment to the Pacific Theater of operations as foot soldiers. After six months training in Australia, the division's first taste of combat came on February 29, 1944, at Los Negros in the Admiralty Islands. The division performed well, inflicting some 7,000 enemy deaths with minor loss of life to the 1st Cav. Their next action found them in Leyte, the main island in the Philippines. General Douglas MacArthur ordered the division to go to Manila and free the prisoners at Santo

Thomas. The next day, the 1st Cav began slicing through 100 miles of Japanese territory and quickly freed Manila and the prisoners, earning MacArthur's naming the Cav as 1st team-first in Manila. At the end of the war, MacArthur gave the 1st team the honor of leading the occupational army into Tokyo, therefore first in Tokyo.

When the North Koreans began invading South Korea, the 1st Cavalry Division was called upon to come to the rescue on July 18, 1950. They landed at Pohangdong, South Korea and began forging north across the 38th parallel, dividing the North from the South. On October 19, 1950, the division captured the capital city of Pyongyang, North Korea. The sudden intervention of communist Chinese forces on October 25th forced all units to retreat to South Korea and defend the important city of Seoul. After much tough fighting, where the 1st Cav continued to prove itself very capable, it returned to Japan where it had been based since the end of WWII. However, on October 15, 1957, the 24th Infantry Division was re-designated the 1st Cavalry Division and became based in South Korea.

When it appeared that the United States would need to take a more prominent military role in Southeast Asia, namely South Vietnam, the 11th Air Assault Division was raised in 1963 at Fort Benning to test airmobile tactics. The colors of the 1st Cavalry Division were flown to Fort Benning and the 11th Air Assault Division's assets transferred to the 1st Cavalry Division. The "air mobile" concept would require new tactics for battle against what was described then as a guerrilla war. This was another first for the 1st Cav. With this new mission came a new weapon– the helicopter. They had been used in Korea, but their full battle potential did not progress until the Vietnam War. President Kennedy saw the importance of this concept with helicopters and wanted to begin building army divisions around their use.

The 1st Cav became the first fully committed American division in the Vietnam War. Their arrival was September 11, 1965, with combat operations beginning in the central highlands of II Corp. By the time the division was withdrawn from Vietnam in the spring of 1971, it had fought in all four regions of the country and demonstrated the effectiveness of the airmobile concept. The bravery of its troopers to not lose a major battle earned a significant amount of awards to individual members. The highest number of Medal of Honor recipients (30) fought for the 1st Cav. Four recipients served with the 5/7. A number of Service Crosses, Silver Stars and Bronze Stars for bravery were awarded to 1st Cav troopers. Because of the tough fighting, many Purple Hearts were also awarded to the numerous members wounded in battle.

7th Cavalry Regiment (Garry Owen)

Army divisions are organized into smaller units called brigades. This was a name change after the Civil War. Cav units continued to use regiment in their terminology, although there was no military organization for a regiment in the Vietnam era. Brigades are made up of even smaller units, known as battalions. Most infantry brigades in Vietnam were assigned four infantry battalions, one artillery battalion, one reconnaissance troop, and a supporting battalion. This meant total brigade strength was 3,500 soldiers.

The 7th Cavalry was a major unit assigned to the 1st Cavalry Division in Vietnam. Its history predates the division by 55 years. It was constituted on July 28, 1866 and organized at Fort Riley, Kansas. It has also been known as the "Garry Owen" Regiment due to the title of a famous Irish beer drinking song that the first commander used for his marching tune. The commander was none other than Colonel George Armstrong Custer, a popular leader during the Civil War. History records what happened to Custer and his troopers at the battle of the Little Big Horn on June 26. 1876. However, from that tragic beginning, the regiment has distinguished itself in further combat as a force that could not be defeated. Most of that fighting has been under the 1st Cavalry Division command. With that legacy, I was extremely fortunate to go to war with one of the best units the army had. Some would even say; "the best."

As the first fully operational division in Vietnam, it didn't seem unrealistic to be the first in battle. There had been some small skirmishes by units of the Cav, the Marines, and others, but the first major battle with the North Vietnamese Army took place in the central highlands in the fall of 1965. The area was called the Ia Drang Valley. The Northern Communist leaders were planning an autumn offensive that would begin in the central highlands and end in Saigon, the capital, thus unifying the two countries. These two formidable enemies collided on Sunday morning, November 14th, when the 1st Battalion, 7th Cavalry, combat assaulted by helicopter into the valley at a landing called LZ X-Ray. After three days of fighting, LZ Albany nearby would be involved on the 17th as well. By the time the entire battle was over, 234 1st Cav troopers had given their lives. But the NVA, with a much larger force, lost many more. They had to recover over 1,800 from the battlefield. A book was published in 1992 that described this battle. "We Were Soldiers Once… And Young," was written by the battalion commander, LTC Hal Moore and a UPI reporter in the battle by the name of Joe Galloway. A movie was made several years later by the same title and used the book to tell the true story of this battle. LTC Moore and Galloway were consultants for this movie. It is one of the best at depicting how combat involves the infantry soldier in battle. There is very little "Hollywood" in this film. It is a very realistic movie of what combat looks like. The bravery, courage, and tenacity of the troopers in this battle not only continued the legacy of the 1st Cav and the 7th Regiment, but also set the bar for the rest of us who followed them in Vietnam.

   This early battle proved that the United States military was in the beginning phase of fighting a very well disciplined, highly trained, tough enemy. The biggest advantage we had was the tremendous support units at our disposal. Had this not been available to LTC Moore and his battalion, they would surely have been wiped out. This was also true for us later in the war. The aerial support from both helicopters and planes was a Godsend. Many times, the artillery fire from firebases helped us to survive enemy attacks. The thought of not having that kind of support when needed would be a very scary one indeed. I have nothing but praise and gratitude for these units who were in dangerous situations themselves, helping us to survive.

**Chapter 4:
Ho Chi Minh Trail**

He who controls the central highlands, controls South Vietnam.
-Vietnamese Military Maxim

The Ho Chi Minh trail was the main road system for the North Vietnamese supplying the Viet Cong in the South. These were South Vietnamese born fighters who believed in Ho Chi Minh and his communist cause. They were very brutal in the way they fought, and it was not unusual to include women and children in their ranks. Sometimes these Viet Cong children would surprise G.I's with a live hand grenade. This road system consisted of a number of trails running north to south through Laos and Cambodia, bordering South Vietnam on its western side. It then branched off into the South, all along the border, giving access to many of the larger population areas. It was named for their long-time leader who died in 1969 while I was there. The trail system started small in the late fifties, nothing more than the widening of a few tribal trails through Laos. North Vietnamese supply troops would head down the trail on foot, mule or bicycle, to support the Viet Cong with weapons, ammunitions, and explosives. This route kept growing and was expanded to a size which allowed trucks to shift supplies down south in greater amounts. Supply depots, medical facilities, and rest stations sprung up along the way, feeding and providing for the thousands of men who would pour down the trail throughout the war. By 1964, the trail was reaching maximum development until the next year when the Russians and Chinese gave North Vietnam road building equipment, which pushed development even farther. The United States made every effort to destroy these series of trails during the war. They were primary targets, but the North Vietnamese were the best in rebuilding the damage and they were never out of usage for long periods of time.

Most of the trail system was shrouded with jungle foliage. It was called "triple canopy" because of the thick growth overhead and all around. The ground foliage was so thick that a machete was needed to cut through. Many times we were cutting a path through the jungle and actually stepped onto a trail before realizing one was there. While rabbit hunting back home during my teen years, I sometimes walked through a thicket that was hard to navigate. But it was nothing compared to the thick foliage of South Vietnam. This was the kind of environment that I would be in during my one-year tour. I found it to be very tough and demanding. With overhead growth, the days appeared cloudy because no direct sunlight could penetrate. This made the nights pitch dark and I could not see my hand in front of my face. The days were hot, although cooler than in the sun, while the night temperature dropped enough for warm covering. The terrain included hills, swamps, creeks, rivers, and rice paddies. There were all kinds of snakes, bugs, and critters. Some of the snakes were highly poisonous; the bamboo viper being one of the most dangerous. It was almost impossible to see because its color matched the bamboo and it was called the "two-step." Supposedly, if bitten, two steps were as far as a person could go. No one in my unit was ever bitten, so I don't know if this is true, but the bite could kill without medical attention. Leeches, especially during the monsoon season, were troublesome. They held on like a tick and sucked blood just the same as a tick or mosquito. And the mosquitos, we used bug repellent, but it didn't seem to help much. Even worse, these mosquitoes carried the dreaded disease malaria. It was not unusual for several guys to get this disease after we would find a bunker complex that the enemy had been using. We were required to take two pills regularly to prevent getting malaria and fortunately, it helped me to escape it. However, in the second month of my tour, one afternoon I began having a very high fever and feeling ill and weak. A monsoon rain helped cool me down and I was allowed to sleep the entire night with no guard duty. The next morning, I felt fine and have always believed I was fighting off malaria. We had found a bunker complex a few days earlier that showed signs of recent activity. This disease became so prevalent in our unit that the company commander ordered all medics to personally watch each of us as we swallowed our pills.

Our main job as an infantry unit was to find the trails that the Viet Cong and NVA used to ferry men and equipment south to wage war against us. Upon finding a well-used trail, we would prepare ambushes to hamper their efforts. The thick jungle foliage provided excellent coverage in which to hide, but the downside was that this was also a benefit to the enemy. They were the best at camouflage and there were times when we actually came within a few feet of an enemy bunker before spotting it. When the enemy was in the bunker, an exchange of gunfire ensued with people on both sides sometimes getting hurt or killed. Bunker complexes were also built along the trails to use as rest areas or places to store food or war materials. There was normally a small hooch on top of the bunker for soldiers to sit and relax. If they were spotted from the air, the soldiers would duck into the bunker to avoid any ordinance or gunfire that might come their way. We usually did not destroy these bunkers ourselves, but threw tear gas grenades into them to prevent the enemy from using them for a period of time.

First Night/Attack?

After my one night on FSB Buttons, I was scheduled to fly out to my unit in a fixed position awaiting re-supply. Before departing, the supply sergeant had given me the essentials I would need in the jungle. I carried an A.L.I.C.E. pack strapped to an aluminum frame with enough c-rations to last until the next log (supply) day. Also in my pack were extra hand grenades and Claymore anti-personnel mines. Attached to my pistol belt and pack were five quarts of water very much needed in this hot tropical environment. I found out very soon that I needed two additional quarts to sustain me between log days. Additional weight included 300 rounds of ammo for my eight-pound M-16 rifle and a very heavy steel helmet on my head. Total weight had to be somewhere between 70 and 80 pounds. Carrying this all day became quite a feat. I guess that's one reason young people fight wars. There's no way I could carry that load now.

After a fifteen-minute flight, we began to circle a small clearing in the jungle. The pilot then made a last-minute descent and landed with great expertise in a very tight clearing cut by members of the company just a short time before. The after-action report states that three log birds were hit by small arms fire supplying A Company July 1st. I do not remember this at all, but the time frame fits with my reporting to my unit. I assume that the report is a typographical error and is meant for another company. However, not yet exposed to hostile gunfire, how would I know unless the rounds were near me?

I immediately reported to the company commander, Captain Tom. I consider him the best of the three that I served with during my tour. He stood 5 feet, 4 inches tall and what he lacked in height was compensated for in his skills as a good leader. He had already served a tour as a platoon leader, giving him the experience to return and command a company. He expected everyone to do their job, but he didn't take unnecessary risks with our lives. He wanted to get everyone home safely and was not trying to earn medals. A combat soldier appreciates a leader like that and would be willing to do whatever his leader orders him to do. Capt. Tom assigned me to the third platoon commanded by Lt. James. He was a college graduate and commissioned through the ROTC program. He was a good leader and well-liked by his platoon. He assigned me to the third squad led by a sergeant from California by the name of Mike. He had been picked in training to attend the NCO academy and had been in the army about six months longer than me. We called these sergeants "shake and bakes," so named because of their quick training and rapid promotion as leaders. In combat, some of them did not measure up, but Mike was a good leader and was promoted to staff sergeant before his tour ended. I didn't know it at the time, but in just a few weeks I would be carrying the squad radio, which meant I would stay near Mike at all times for him to communicate with the platoon leader and company commander. We developed a close relationship during this time and respected each other's ability to perform our duty in extreme conditions. In fact, this was true with each squad member. We trusted each other with our lives and that kind of relationship formed a bond among us like no other. The phrase "band of brothers" from WWII rings true. This bond still lasts with us today.

These brothers-in-arms became my best friends and I love them like a brother. Two squad members rotated home a few weeks after my arrival, so I really didn't get to know them. We were all young soldiers representing the country from one coast to the other. Big Ed, from Michigan, was the tallest and looked like the oldest with his bald head. He returned home for a death in his family during his tour and did not return to us. Jerry was a replacement, and one of the ones who contracted malaria early in his tour and also did not return. Bob, Mike, and Neil came to the squad a few weeks after me. Bob was from Maryland and liked to bet on horse races. He received a racing magazine in the mail on a regular basis. He became one of the best point men we had, Neil was a Connecticut native, very reserved, and a good soldier. Mike, from Minnesota, didn't have much to say like Neil, but was also a good soldier. Bill (Florida) and Jack (Massachusetts) were veteran squad members and helped us new guys from the start. Harold, from North Carolina and Johnny from Georgia, became my closest buddies. They also had been members of the squad for many months. The remaining member was Burley from Oklahoma, who came to us shortly after my arrival. We also became very close and were very similar in our lifestyles, even though we lived miles apart. Burley and Johnny would be seriously wounded in the October 20 ambush, spending a long time both in and out of the hospital recovering from their wounds. They are considered one hundred percent disabled by the Veterans Administration. Working closely with other squads, we also became very much a band of brothers with some of them. Their names were: Terry, Mike, Harold, Jack, Steve, Ed, Lenny, Alabama (John), Rudy, Chuck, and Bo. We were a team willing to help each other.

3rd squad, 3rd platoon members (Dagenhart bottom row, 2nd from right)

Everybody in the squad had to take turns on perimeter guard, usually one hour each night. Being the new guy, squad leader Mike pulled his guard time and also stayed awake with me during my turn this first night. There were no problems during my guard, but the strange jungle noises intrigued me, especially a lizard. When this lizard called in the night, it sounded just like someone saying "f... you". This tended to be a constant joke among us. We were not near a trail, but sometime in the night everyone was awakened for full alert. There was movement outside our perimeter. All weapons were locked and loaded with everyone ready to defend their positions. I don't remember being afraid, but I really didn't know enough to be fearful. I found out quickly that fear is a constant in combat. I saw very few men who were not afraid, even leaders. However, we tried not to show our fear and our training helped to overcome it. The movement became more intense, and it was hard to tell how many individuals were there. In combat, sometimes a person's mind thinks of things in the extreme. I'm sure many of us thought we were facing a large enemy unit; maybe even thinking we would not live to see a new day. We even heard pigs squealing with this movement. We assumed Charlie (Viet Cong) was bringing fresh meat with him for food. Finally, the movement stopped. Silence is sometimes worse than noise. Were they on top of us? Were they moving to another part of our perimeter to attack? Would we make it through the night? After some time of this silence, we realized that whoever or whatever the movement was had disappeared. The remainder of the night was uneventful.

Our squad was tasked with checking the area of the movement as daylight began. Our two-point men approached this site very slowly, not knowing what they might find. Not more than 25 or 30 yards from our night's perimeter these men threw their weapons into the air and started slapping themselves like wild men. They ran forward several more yards and just disappeared. It looked as if the earth had swallowed them. Other members of the squad began to cautiously move to the spot where the point men were last seen. Once there, they were immediately stung by a number of yellow jackets. The mystery was solved. Instead of a large enemy unit, the movement from the night before was a group of wild hogs who had disturbed that nest of bees. The point men who disappeared; they had fallen into a ravine when they ran forward. Although no enemy contact happened, this really makes a good war story to embellish when sitting around the bar or fireplace making conversation.

Under Fire

The company moved out soon after discovering the bees and relocated to an area that battalion wanted a small firebase built. Engineers had already cleared the spot with dozers and pushed up a three-foot-high berm forming a circular perimeter. They also dug holes for bunkers, but we would be responsible for filling sandbags and placing defensive wire around the base. I don't remember placing the wire because we left this base within a week or two. But the war became a reality for me on this small base on our second day there. Late in the afternoon, I was able to secure five gallons of water to use for a quick shower. Our company had been in the jungle for thirty plus days and no one had a chance to bathe in that time. Here I was in my third day in the bush and I thought I needed a bath! I would learn very quickly that a daily bath is not in an infantry battalion headquarters SOP. The mission always took precedence over everything else. It was not unusual to spend days and weeks without the luxury of a bath, or clean clothes. This has made me appreciate more the little things that we take for granted each day. Our body odor had to be terrible, but all in candor, we hardly noticed it among ourselves. However, those who were confined on the firebases did not want to be anywhere near us until we had the opportunity to bathe.

With my bath water in a military canvas bag made specifically for that purpose, I was lathered down and in the process of rinsing when suddenly a mortar round landed just outside the opposite side of the perimeter. The next one landed on the same line of sight just inside the perimeter. This round was a direct hit on our military utility vehicle called a mule. It was similar to the present-day all-terrain vehicle. The mortar totally destroyed our mule. The next round hit farther inside the perimeter, again on the same line of sight, but heading right for me. The enemy was very good at walking mortars in line like that and I realized in just a few seconds the next rounds would land around or on top of me. I started for the bunker, but must not have been quick enough because one of my squad buddies actually grabbed me and threw me into the bunker. I didn't have time for clothes and the bunker walls and floor consisted of red dirt, just like back home. I was still wet from the shower and the bath I had taken was a waste of time because I was covered with this dirt. Boy, was I ticked off! I think I was madder about being bathed in the dirt than the enemy trying to kill me. Approximately twenty rounds landed inside the base with no injuries except to our mule. I'm sure I didn't get hurt because of my buddy's action that afternoon. Harold would guide me and protect me like a mother hen in my first weeks and I believe his concern kept me alive until I gained some combat experience. Harold became my closest buddy and we still get together frequently after all these years. Our homes were only forty miles apart but today, he lives farther away in a nearby state. From this third day in combat to the end of my tour one year later, I would learn to hate mortars with a passion. Without overhead cover, almost impossible in the jungle, there is no defense against this weapon of war. I never overcame the fear of them.

With Harold (right) at FSB Mary

We prepared our defense for the rest of the afternoon and night expecting more mortars and a ground attack. Thankfully, the enemy must have just wanted us to know they were in the neighborhood because we had an uneventful night. The next morning our platoon was sent out to find the location of the mortar fire. We had not gone far into the jungle when we located a small trail. We followed this trail in one direction for some distance without finding anything. However, we retraced our steps and followed the trail in the opposite direction, quickly finding the spot where the mortars had been fired. Also found at the spot were two bicycles used to haul the mortar tube and base plate. This would not be the last time we found bicycles used for enemy transportation. They could tie hundreds of pounds of equipment or rice on a bicycle and push it many miles down the trail to its destination.

On the afternoon of July 8th, the 1st platoon engaged an individual with small arms fire on a well-used trail, resulting in one enemy KIA. He was carrying a pack containing U.S. fragmentation grenades. The next few weeks brought very little activity, except several firefights by our sister companies B and D. We certainly didn't get mad about the enemy taking a break.

They were evidently still recovering from the tremendous losses during the Big Tet Offensive the year before. We would find out that this enemy could still bring a good fight without the numbers they had prior to Tet. They had already blooded the company in the months prior to my arrival. August and September would bring more enemy activity for the entire battalion and even with the turnover in replacements; we had a large number of combat veterans in our company. They would help us new guys to become seasoned veterans in the weeks ahead.

Fear Factor

Like all kids growing up, there were things that frightened me; the dark of night, some animals, loud noises, and some adults, who seemed to be intimidating. As I grew older though, things like these were not so scary. But combat is in a league of its own. I have never been more frightened than the one year of duty I spent in the jungles of South Vietnam. Although death was a real possibility, I was more afraid of losing limbs, suffering brain damage, or losing my ability to produce children than my death.

There were a few men who could not handle the hostile environment of infantry combat. With the constant stress of small arms fire, RPGs, mortars, and rockets, the training they had could not overcome the fear they faced. This does not mean they were cowards. On the contrary, this usually happened with a new guy who was exposed to heavy contact before having a chance to get some experience in small firefights. As a new replacement, he didn't know anyone, felt very much alone, and was facing something for the first time that was so brutal and unimaginable that he simply could not function as trained.

Although fear was always present, I admit that during the battle, whether big or small, the adrenaline was flowing producing a high that must be similar to a drug high. I cannot deny that I liked that feeling. After the fight, with emotions and senses at such a high, all energy was drained from my body.

Having been in combat, seeing the worst of mankind and being frightened by it all, now living in my senior years, very few things frighten me anymore.

Chapter 5:
FSB Perimeter Guard

Infantrymen, who spend their time in combat being shelled, strafed, and shot at,
walking gingerly through minefields, and sleeping in muddy holes in the ground,
are always inordinately grateful for the small comforts
that most civilians take for granted.
-Flint Whitlock, The Fighting First

    The small bases that we used for support to patrol the jungle provided the immediate help we needed when we got into more trouble than we thought we could handle. The ratio of support to infantry was about ten to one. This did not mean just fire support. It included clerical, logistics, medical, and other jobs related to the entire mission of the war. During my tour, approximately 540,000 personnel were in country, but only 50,000 to 60,000 were grunts in the jungles, villages, and rice paddies confronting the enemy. More than 70 percent of all casualties were suffered by the infantry and this was two and a half times higher than those suffered in World War II. There were usually 105 MM artillery pieces located on the base. If the base was larger, it also included 155 MM howitzers. Sometimes other weapons would be attached to provide extra security for the firebase itself. Patrolling around these bases, we were very seldom out of range of their guns. One of the companies always served as perimeter guard 24/7. Battalion rotated each company into the base for a one or two-week guard duty while the other companies continued patrolling. This was a time to get baths and clean clothes and be able to ease some stress of constant patrolling against a formidable enemy. Although these bases were subject to attack at any time, they provided a measure of security not found in the jungle. The company providing perimeter guard was kept busy during the day filling sandbags or enhancing the defensive posture of the base itself. This break from patrolling was a good morale booster and gave us grunts a small taste of more normal living conditions. We were able to have more hot meals available instead of the day-to-day c-rations. Although we were sleeping on the ground, we had dry hooches with sandbag overhead cover protecting us from mortars. We could even use lighting at night if the light was concealed enough to prevent making a target for the enemy. This small measure of normalcy was highly appreciated by us grunts.

Returning from patrol with Squad Leader Mike (right)

Activity in August began on the second by finding 12,400 pounds of rice packaged in 200-pound bags. The next day we found another 6,200 pounds in the same general area. These caches were not being guarded at the time. The rice had been taken from the Vietnamese farmers and hidden by the Viet Cong. We contacted the battalion and they made sure it was redistributed to the Vietnamese people. Rice, along with fish, was the staple diet of these people, so they were very pleased to get their rice returned. Continuing to patrol in this area, we found a large bunker complex with military equipment in storage. Twelve bicycles, 14 mines, 97 rifles, and a 51-caliber machine gun were found without any enemy resistance. Now this is the way to fight a war!

By August 12th, Alpha Company was authorized a three day stand down. This meant we would be taken from the jungle to a large base with amenities almost like home. Showers, clean clothes, with no guard duty required during our stay would be the order of the day. We would have a good time eating, drinking, sleeping, just taking it easy doing what we wanted to do, within reason, of course. These type of stand downs were the only times that our weapons were taken from us. We were just getting settled in for our first night free of combat when "Charlie" decided to crash our party. Elements of the 1st and 7th NVA divisions and the 5th and 9th VC divisions attacked 1st Cav Division bases throughout III Corp. We were located at our brigade headquarters in Quan Loi. At 1:20 AM these enemy troops attacked the perimeter with a well-trained sapper platoon. They knocked out two bunkers, killing most of the guys on guard in these bunkers. The attack continued into the heart of the base, where the village of Quan Loi was located. The enemy killed the village chief and his young daughter.

The entire company was put on alert, given our weapons and ammo with orders to report to the perimeter where the attack started. We took positions on the berm spaced about four feet apart, ready for any further assault by the enemy. In the military, even taking the best precautions, accidents will happen. Not long after taking our positions, a terrible event happened that almost took the life of one of our guys. Just a few days before, two new guys came to us as replacements. This was their first chance at combat action and I'm sure they were just as afraid as we had been as new troopers. They were placed side by side on the berm and told to leave their headgear on their heads. In front of us between the berm and wire lay a number of dead VC from the attack. They did not wear headgear and the new guys could see their bodies just over the berm from them. One of the new guys evidently forgot the order about his headgear and removed his steel pot. The other new guy near him saw his friend's silhouette and fired several shots at him with his M-16, thinking he was another VC sneaking over the berm. One round just barely grazed the side of the new trooper's head, just above the ear. The other rounds missed, causing great relief once we knew what happened. However, this near miss affected both of these guys. The soldier fired upon was so shaken that the first firefight several days later caused him to freeze. He could not react as trained and was placed in another job at headquarters. The trooper doing the shooting was upset but recovered and became one of the best point men we had.

Thankfully, the attack was over, but we still maintained perimeter guard at the bunkers the remainder of the night. At daylight, all platoons of A Company reconnoitered inside the base following the path of attack. We found more enemy dead along with grenades and Bangalore torpedoes discarded between the perimeter and the village. This is when we found the bodies of the village chief and his daughter, who looked to be 8 or 9 years old. Seeing children murdered by an enemy that did not value the lives of innocents in war was hard to accept. Most of us did not hate our enemy but this certainly made it easy to do so. After this, our platoon reconnoitered outside the base looking for other enemy dead or wounded. We didn't patrol very far into the jungle before approaching a Viet Cong sitting against a tree. He was wearing no clothing and was literally burned from his head to his feet. He was probably one of the sappers who evidently was burned from a barrel of phougas buried and blown by one of the guys on guard in the bunker at the beginning of the attack. He was burned so badly that I didn't see how he was still living. A helicopter was called out to pick him up for treatment and questioning. We patrolled the area for a little longer with no further findings and returned to base to continue our stand down.

Being able to finish our stand down was a great morale booster. A few days later, we returned to the jungle around Quan Loi searching for the bad guys who attacked the base. On August 24th, we found the graves of six NVA soldiers, probably involved in the recent night attack. Continuing to recon the area, a small firefight erupted with one of our guys wounded, but two enemy were killed. The next day we made contact with an unknown enemy force in bunkers. We received fire from small arms, machine guns, RPGs, and returned fire with our weapons and support from our mortar platoon. Aerial and fixed artillery also came to our aid. After the fight, only two NVA bodies were found, but several blood trails lead from the bunkers. A large amount of munitions was found here. None of us were hurt in this fight.

On the 26th we found an extensive abandoned bunker complex that appeared to be a training center. Inside this complex was a 40-meter-wide mock-up that looked like FSB Buttons, our big base. Using this training center "Charlie" did attack Buttons in early November. After a two-hour assault, enemy losses were substantial with few casualties on our side.

During this early part of my tour, we had orders for a combat assault into an area of rice paddies. The weather was perfect and the sun was shining brightly on that day. If I remember correctly, we began loading on the helicopters mid-morning with a twenty-minute flight for my first experience in rice country. It was the growing season, but the rice stalks were still flooded with approximately two feet of water. The pilots chose to hover above the paddy for us to exit the chopper. With my weight and heavy gear, my legs sunk to my knees in the mud of this water. I could not move an inch without help from my buddies. A sniper would have had ample time to shoot me right there in that paddy. That would have been a bad way to start the day, but I don't remember any contact with the enemy on this mission.

RTO (Radio Telephone Operator)

I began my tour as a rifleman like most infantrymen in Vietnam and took my turn walking point. This meant that I would be at the point of contact in most firefights at very close range to the enemy. I didn't look forward to this, but it was my job that fate handed me and I tried to be ready. There were no safe places to be in the jungle but walking point was one of the most dangerous. As a grunt, all of us had to use our senses just like an animal guarding against his survival. Any movement, anything that did not look normal, was a warning that danger was near. If the point man missed this, the unit had a chance of being ambushed or taking casualties from booby traps. I never enjoyed walking point. Later I decided to carry the M-79 grenade launcher, but sometime in August, I started carrying the squad radio. It became available when my buddy, Harold, became one of the company commander's radio operators. I found this to be my calling in combat. Having a radio allowed me to be more aware of things happening with the platoon and company. Most guys didn't want to carry the extra 25 pounds and the extra attention it brought from enemy gunners. Eliminating communications was always a tactic used by both sides. AND I DIDN'T LIKE WALKING POINT! I was pretty good using the radio and it would be my job the remainder of my tour. The last three months I would be one of several operators working in the battalion TOC (tactical operations center).

I began my radio career putting it in jeopardy almost immediately. After finding the enemy training center, we engaged some individuals in a bunker near a trail late in the afternoon. For some reason, this engagement is not mentioned in the action reports. Darkness fell before we could continue the fight, so we pulled back, set up a NDP, with plans to attack the next morning. At daylight we attacked the bunker once again, with lighter resistance than the day before. It still took about an hour to fight our way into the area. We had stumbled into another large complex that the enemy was not willing to stay and protect. Most of them had left the area only leaving behind a small unit to keep us busy for a while. There was a central location of bunkers (approximately twenty) with separate trails leading from these to other bunkers in five different directions. In searching the whole complex, Mike and I became separated from the other guys in the squad. Just the two of us started down a trail thinking we would be joining the other guys in our squad. Approximately 100 yards from the central complex, we came to another group of bunkers (ten or twelve). It appeared that no one was home, and Mike wanted to check these out for himself. He told me to cover him as he searched each bunker. I tried to talk him out of this because I could call on the radio for others to come to our location. A sniper could have easily ended our day at that moment. He insisted and proceeded slowly to check all of them. Thankfully, the enemy was gone, but I felt we were taking a risk that was not needed and told him so. In fact, I told him that if he did something like this again, I would not be at his side. He did not chastise me, so I guess he realized the danger we were in and did not do anything after this that I felt should be questioned. After the company thoroughly searched the entire complex, the platoons were ordered to begin patrolling out beyond the bunkers while waiting for a demolition team to come and destroy them. The team had just begun their work when we heard several mortars being dropped in their tubes not far from us. Hearing the mortars being fired is a scary feeling because there is no way to know where they will land. No noise can be heard from their falling out of the sky. These landed in the central bunker location with one of the demolition team members being killed. We had to carry his body to a small clearing where a helicopter could land to get him back for his return home. No one else was hurt and this would be the last shot at us before the remaining enemy left the area.

September began as a quiet month. This may have been the time when our squad was required to set up farther down the trail as a listening post for the night. We were near a South Vietnamese outpost who heard our movement and began lobbing M-79 rounds among us in the listening post. Had there been mortars, I'm sure we could have been killed or wounded. No one was hurt by the rounds, but it took several minutes to communicate with the Vietnamese to stop their firing. I also remember our squad being sent down a trail some distance on another occasion to recon for the entire company. This was one of those times when I felt strongly that we were being watched with every step on the trail. To this day, I have no way of knowing because we made no contact and saw nothing unusual.

North Vietnam's longtime communist leader, Ho Chi Minh, died on September 2nd. The enemy initiated a three-day ceasefire that didn't make us mad at all. By the tenth, the NVA decided it was time for war again and began a mortar barrage on our Charlie Company. On the 12th, my 23rd birthday, we were working the jungle in close proximity to our D Company when both companies made contact with an enemy unit. In the middle of the fight, a very handsome looking enemy soldier got caught between our two companies. Seeing no way out except his being killed, he surrendered to one of our A Company platoons. In questioning we found him to be a regimental staff officer who provided a lot of good information to the Intel guys at battalion. He did not appear to be 100% Vietnamese. His facial features and larger size made us think he may be the offspring of a French soldier during their war with the North Vietnamese in the fifties. He was taken out by a helicopter to be questioned further. We never found out if he was part French.

Continuing to recon the area, we found an intersection where two trails came together, forming a T. This is where we set up our NDP with our squad at the T intersection. The machine gun was placed here with claymore mines and trip flares positioned up the trails. We checked and rechecked our defenses because of the contact earlier in the day. We expected that the enemy was still in the area and may want revenge for the capture of one of their officers. We would not be disappointed. At 10:30 PM, (I had just laid down to sleep) the trip flare placed up the trail ignited, and night changed to day for a brief time. To my surprise, kneeling on the trail less than ten yards from me, (I was in the next position from the machine gun) was a VC. Mike was at the machine gun and reached to blow the claymore, but it would not explode. The next morning, we found that the kneeling soldier had cut the wire to the mine, just as the trip flare fired. Mike opened up with the machine gun while several of us fired our M-16s at AK-47 fire from the trail behind the kneeling soldier. If more Viet Cong were nearby, they didn't stay any longer because enemy fire ceased very quickly and all became quiet again. We knew that the enemy would know our location now. This is a scary position to be in, especially with no more mines or trip flares on the trail of attack. Line companies in our battalion did not move in the jungle at night, it was too dangerous. With this contact, we expected to be attacked again during the night. We spent the rest of the night on full alert and I wondered if my foxhole was deep enough. I was not particularly pleased with all this excitement on my birthday but, thankfully, the rest of the night was peaceful.

    During that brief action, I witnessed what I considered to be a strange reaction from the kneeling soldier who cut our wire. When the trip flare fired and lighted the trail, this guy didn't fall to the ground and try to crawl away as expected. He immediately stood up, looking very tall, making an excellent target and it cost him his life. His two buddies up the trail firing their AKs at us didn't live to see another day either. The next morning, we searched their bodies for intel. I kept a small cigarette lighter and a hammock, found on one of the bodies. Later, I gave the hammock to Mike. I could not sleep in it because it was just not comfortable for me. Some guys liked hammocks because it usually kept bugs and other critters from crawling on them.

    On September 15th, B Company engaged a force estimated to include two NVA companies. One of our helicopter support units came to their aid. Later in the battle we were also called upon for support and entered the fight near the end. We also conducted a sweep of the area finding 14 NVA bodies and numerous blood trails. A large amount of military equipment and ammunition was found in the contact area. Four days later, our platoon saw smoke while moving down a trail. We hurriedly set up an ambush waiting for something to develop. Soon an individual was sighted carrying a weapon and was fired upon and killed. Our "rules of engagement" in the jungle were very liberal. Civilians knew to stay out of the jungle. Only American GIs and the enemy used the jungle. So we often had the opportunity to shoot first, thereby increasing our chances of survival. The troops who had to work the villages did not have that luxury. Killing an innocent civilian would bring murder charges to a soldier. This was made more difficult in villages because it was impossible at times to know who the enemy was. The Viet Cong did not wear military uniforms. They dressed just like the other Vietnamese people. The dead VC was carrying an American made M-1 carbine and wearing a watch that he had bought in the village of Song Be. He may have been the barber or a store owner in the village. This was true in a lot of cases; in the day they appeared to be a friend, but at night they tried to end your life.

    The time frame is not clear, but sometime in this month, battalion sent a military dog team to assist us. These service dogs were usually German Shepherds or Labrador Retrievers trained and assigned for different duty. The very aggressive ones became sentry dogs. The less aggressive and highly intelligent were trained for scout duty in various roles. The Labradors, having very sensitive noses, went to tracker school. All were trained at Lackland Air Force Base in Texas before assigned duty. A four-digit number was tattooed in their left ear for identification purposes. Over 4,000 served with courage and distinction in Vietnam and Thailand. Approximately 350 were killed in action, with many more wounded. Two hundred sixty-three handlers lost their lives while working with their dogs. Fewer than two hundred dogs came back to the states because this was the policy followed by the military in that day. I remember that a dog and handler came to us by helicopter on a log day and patrolled with us the rest of the day without making contact with the enemy. The next day we did make contact with a small force. The dog alerted his handler properly but would not listen to his commands and chased after the enemy. Unfortunately, the dog got in the crossfire and was shot by our guys. The handler was very upset and I understood his reaction, but human lives were on the line. Our guys were sorry that it happened, but certainly did not purposely intend to take the dog's life. He was picked up by helicopter and buried with honors, just as any military person would have been. There were several other times dogs were used with us, but I don't remember anything significant that happened.

    Again, the time is not clear, but sometime in September I moved from the squad to the command post. I would no longer be Mike's RTO or be with my squad buddies all day and night. I would miss being with them, but would still see them regularly. The company commander asked me to carry the radio being used on the company frequency. This kept him in contact with his platoon leaders and their squads. I would be back with my buddy Harold, who was carrying the other company radio tuned to the battalion frequency.

I'll never forget what Capt. Tom asked about accepting his offer. He emphasized that I needed to be within arms- length of him at all times in the bush because he had to be in communication with his platoons in any firefight. He also said that there would be times that he would have to go to the point of contact in order to deploy the troops in stopping the attack. He said he didn't need me if I could not do this. My first thought was that my mom and wife would probably not like that arrangement, but I decided to tell him I would be his shadow. I silently vowed to not disappoint him and as previously stated he was a very good leader and well respected by everyone in the company. Carrying the radio and being in close personal contact with him gave me a great perspective of his leadership and honest personality. He proved this early on when we were sent on a day patrol in an area of suspected enemy activity. Since we were to be picked up later in the day, we traveled light, meaning no packs and only one meal. When we began looking for an open area to bring in helicopters, we searched diligently, but could only find one large enough for one chopper. The battalion commander was in his command helicopter telling Capt. Tom that if we had searched in a direction he could see 1500 feet in the air, we could have found a PZ (pick-up zone). Capt. Tom finally was irritated and told his boss that we did the best we could in the thick jungle we were patrolling. Unfortunately, we had to spend the night sleeping on the ground without air mattresses and cover for the cool temperature. It was a very long and uncomfortable night, but we found no enemy and I believe we did find a clearing the nest day and returned to base. The battalion commander did go back and bring out c-rations for us. His pilot lowered the helicopter within 15 to 20 feet of the ground and meals were dropped out to us. It was a tight clearing but the pilot proved our case that we could be taken out that afternoon. I was not very happy with our commander. I'm sure he was called various names by the troopers after he left.

Tom, Company Commander. A great leader.

Chapter 6:
Hell on Earth

*True courage is the willingness to give up
all that is dear when living is most precious.*
     Pericles, Athenian Statesman

I had no way of knowing at the time, but October would be the month with the most enemy activity, and the 20th would forever be the worst day of my life. Almost fifty years later, my bad days in life have been nothing compared to that day in October. In fact, I've occasionally said that a bad day here in the states would have been a good day in combat in Vietnam. We lost more guys in this month than any other time on my tour. True courage was never more visible than at this critical juncture in our company's history. I know that at least eight Silver Stars (3rd highest for valor) were awarded, three of them posthumously. This has been the hardest part of this memoir to write. The memory of the events only brings sadness because of combat brothers lost and those others whose lives have been altered from serious wounds of battles.

October 1st, 1969, became the warning for larger things brewing. I don't know for sure, but I suspect we were still dealing with some of the same enemy units from the September contact. We continued to work the jungle out of our large base, FSB Buttons. On this day at dawn, we were surprised by thirty rounds of 82 MM mortars and a ground assault against our perimeter where the second platoon was located. Using AK-47s, RPGs, and grenades, the NVA unit wounded twelve guys, including the platoon leader, Steve. His injuries were serious enough to send him home. Gary, one of our medics trying to help the wounded, was himself seriously hurt and died twenty-three days later. There was a break in the mortars, but a short time later, thirty-five rounds of 60 MM mortars landed inside our perimeter. Even in this chaos, our NCOs lead their squads to provide heavy return fire, using support from our company mortar platoon and artillery from FSB Buttons. Sgt. Ed, Sgt. Tom, Spec. 4 Denny, and Pfc. Melvin, received Silver Stars for their courageous actions that morning. Twelve Bronze Stars were also awarded for the battle. The enemy was not through; a medevac helicopter called to take out our wounded received ground-to-air fire but made it back to base. After the fight, a sweep was made of the area, finding a number of dead NVA and blood trails leading to bunkers with ten more enemy KIAs and weapons. The next day, we spotted one NVA on a trail and engaged him with small arms fire, killing him and capturing his AK-47.

  The next two weeks saw a number of individuals from villages in our area of operations surrender to troops at FSB Buttons and several smaller bases. Some of these people claimed to be VC. On the 16th, two of these villagers walked into our position carrying no weapons. Two days later, we found an empty bunker complex and a grave containing two enemy KIAs. They very well could have been involved in the October 1st action. The company was picked up this day (18th) and inserted into an area 13 miles northeast of Buttons, where a B-52 strike was initiated just a night or two before. Brigade knew that enemy activity was strong in this area and wanted a line company to do a BDA (bomb damage assessment). This meant patrolling the bombed area to confirm possible target destruction.

  Brigade intelligence had intercepted radio transmissions on four enemy radio stations within 5 kilometers of the strike. One was identified as a regimental headquarters, one a battalion, one a heavy weapons company, and the fourth was unidentified. If these units were still in the area, we would be very much outnumbered and outgunned. I've often wondered why our headquarters sent just one understrength company of 100 men into this area with the Intel they had at the time. I could only conclude that we were evidently used as bait to lure the enemy out of their hiding places. It also leads me to believe that higher command was willing to risk sacrificing an entire company in order to locate and destroy the NVA units with more B-52 strikes. None of this was known to us at the time and two days later we would suffer horribly for the unsuccessful bombing mission and the terrible decision to send just us into the area. The entire battalion should have been deployed on this mission.

God Help Us

We found the bombed area shortly after being dropped off by the helicopters. This may have been the time when I had to jump from the high side as the chopper hovered near the crest of a hill. I had to jump from 10 feet or more, but was not hurt. We realized very quickly that the bomb run missed the intended target. Continuing to search, we felt that contact with the enemy was very possible. We needed an open area for pickup a couple of days later, so we looked for one as we patrolled. A small opening was spotted, but we felt it could not be enlarged very much by us. It resulted in the only one available, so we made plans to remove several trees with explosives, but were still hampered by its small size. It would only be large enough for two helicopters, not the normal six.

After patrolling for the remainder of the day without making contact, we settled in for the night next to this clearing to begin enlarging the next morning. My memory tells me that one of the platoons started working on clearing soon after sunrise while the others began patrolling the area. The company commander and his RTOs (Jim and I) accompanied one of the platoons on patrol and quickly found a small, recently cut trail with communication wire crossing it. This caused us some concern because the wire meant that these enemy units were probably connected together by land line. Later, an NVA officer unsuspectingly walked up to the platoon's trailing guard. The alert trooper killed this guy and searched his rucksack, finding binoculars. Evidently, he was the FO (forward observer) for an enemy mortar or artillery unit. This only increased our concern because this was the first sighting of the enemy despite all the patrolling from the day before. They were well hidden and wanted to fight us when they were ready.

We ended the day doing something we had never done before and did not do again during my tour. We set up for the night again in the same location beside the clearing. An infantry unit should never use the same location two nights in a row. Even if we moved only one hundred yards, we moved to prevent the enemy from knowing our night location. This would be the dumbest mistake made in my tour. Continued activity on the small PZ would also be a detriment to our safety. Capt. Tom left the company after the battle of October 1st for a brigade position to finish his tour. He was replaced by Capt. Gary, who had also commanded a platoon in his first tour. Normally the CO makes the decision for night defensive positions. However, I don't remember if battalion command gave him any instructions to stay in the same place. Regardless of who made it, this decision haunts all of us many years later who lived through it. This was one of those tragic events in combat that is never erased from one's mind. For those troopers wounded, their reminder comes from the pain and suffering they endure every day of their lives.

  The next morning (the 20th) began with additional clearing of the PZ. The battalion commander ordered the supply officer to send a couple of chainsaws out to us to clear the trees. There has been a misconception about this with many of our guys thinking Capt. Gary requested these saws. In fact, the Capt. didn't want them. I was monitoring the radio and heard the statement by the S4 (supply officer) that the battalion CO ordered the saws brought out. The S4 even argued against it. In spite of the noise from the saws, I firmly believe the NVA knew exactly where we were and what we were doing. There was simply too much activity by us in this location. I was not comfortable with our situation. My fear level was reaching new highs. I just knew that things did not look good for us. We were in an area of heavy enemy activity that a B-52 strike did not eliminate; we could not find our enemy even with signs pointing to their presence; we were in one spot too long; and our means of escape were critical because the size of our PZ was too small.

  By 3:00 PM, all patrols returned to our perimeter and the PZ was ready for the helicopters. Soon the choppers arrived and the first two landed in our small clearing. This is one of the most dangerous moments for the helicopters, waiting for the grunts to jump on if ambushed. It's also a bad moment for the small number of grunts still on the ground waiting for the last lift, if being attacked. The new CO, Jim, and I, were standing just inside the perimeter in the edge of the clearing when approximately 25-30 mortars exploded near our night's command post location. They actually landed in the middle of our own mortar platoon. Spec. 4 James Aldred, Spec. 4 Michael Dagnon, PFC Jose Ortiz, Spec. 4 Alexander Vigil, and Spec. 4 David Brannon died from these mortars. I don't believe anyone in the mortar platoon escaped injury. Some of the shrapnel landed around us with the CO and Jim catching a piece or two. Their wounds weren't serious and I still don't understand how I was missed. This would happen several times during my tour, and I don't have an explanation for this.

The NVA's timing was perfect. I believe their mortars were intended to destroy the helicopters. They didn't miss their mark by very much. While these mortars were doing their damage, a ground attack began on the opposite side of the perimeter against 3rd platoon. Just a few weeks before, I was a member of this platoon. If this had happened then, I would have been in the middle of this fight. Defending against numerous NVA using AK-47s, RPGs, and machine guns, four more of our brothers were killed. They were Cpl. James Coleman, PFC Albert Davis, Cpl. Charles Edwards, and Sgt. Martin Essary, Jr. Davis and Edwards received Silver Stars posthumously. Many more were injured, some very seriously. Two of the badly wounded were a couple of my best buddies from my former squad. Burley received six rounds from an AK-47 with the most serious injury to his throat. Johnny was shot through the upper arm where the round continued down the side of his body, exiting near his knee. I really don't see how these guys survived, but the medics did their miraculous jobs under tremendous enemy fire. Our senior medic, Steve, received his Silver Star for actions on that day.

I felt guilty for many years about Burley's injuries that day. When I left the squad to carry the company radio for the CO, I convinced him to take the squad radio. I thought carrying a radio in the field could possibly lead to a better job out of the jungle and to a more secure location such as a firebase. Burley did not want any part of carrying a radio, but eventually changed his mind. After the 20th, I blamed myself for almost causing his death. Again, had this happened while I was still in the squad, I would have taken the rounds. I believed he took the shots meant for me. I visited with him in his home several times before I had the courage to bring this up. He relieved my years of guilt by telling me that I was not responsible for his injuries and that he didn't even hate the NVA soldier who shot him. I would do anything for these two buddies who still suffer from their wounds on that terrible day.

During an insertion or pick-up there was always aerial support with the Cobra gunships as well as artillery available. We desperately needed both that day. Once the gunships used all their firepower and returned to base to rearm, we called on artillery support from near-by firebases. This additional support was effective, but like any sustained battle, we continued to receive fire and had men dying that needed to be taken out. The CO was on the company radio talking to his platoon leaders, but appeared to be confused about what to do. First Sgt. Leo realized this and made his way to the point of contact. He provided the leadership needed and kept us organized in this very tough fight. I was busy on the battalion radio communicating with the helicopter pilots and our artillery forward observer on the ground with us. Harold had been reassigned to headquarters as a battalion radio operator just a few days before, so I changed to the battalion frequency to replace him. The artillery observer was adjusting fire for maximum effect. There was no way a chopper could take out our wounded until the artillery fire was stopped. If the decision was made to end this firing and bring in a medevac, it faced the possibility of taking fire and its pilots and crew could be killed. If artillery support ended too soon, more people on the ground faced the same possible outcome. In the chaos of battle, decisions have to be made quickly. There is no time to call a committee together. We did eventually get our wounded safely out of the battle. Could more have been saved if decisions had been made differently? I don't believe anyone there that day could answer that question with certainty. I just know that all of us did a tremendous job in that battle facing terrible odds. Without the help of our artillery and the gunships, I believe we would have been overrun and the company destroyed. I'm certain this is when I decided that I would not allow the NVA or Viet Cong to capture me. I would take my own life before being subjected to their inhumane treatment and torture.

105mm Howitzer support

155mm Howitzer support

Cobra Gunship

    I was so busy on the radio that I have no idea how long this battle lasted, but we did get removed before sunset. At the end of the day, I realized that I had not fired a shot in this, the biggest fight in my tour. But I didn't need to; it was being handled by some of the bravest guys I know. I will never forget the fearless way they fought that day. I flew out on a helicopter with several of our KIAs. I don't have the words to describe my feelings as I looked at these young men (youngest was 19) who had sacrificed everything. Just hours before, they were laughing and joking and very much alive. Now they would not see another day. Future dreams for their lives would never happen. They would not see old age or be able to play with grandchildren. Their families would be heartbroken when notified by the visit of a Chaplain and his Army escort. It became very real to me that day that freedom is not "free". It comes with a very high price. As we exited the chopper at a firebase, I noticed a cigarette lighter among the bodies. It belonged to Sgt. Essary. His name was engraved on it. It was a 1st Cav lighter given to him as "Sky Trooper" of the month during his tour. I made sure it was placed with his personal effects so that his family would receive it. Martin was a squad leader and had just a few short weeks before his tour ended.

I would be remiss if I didn't give the Air Force recognition for their support that day as well. Those F4 Phantoms provided three air strikes dropping heavy ordinance on the bad guys. This is one of several times during my tour that we asked for their help and they responded quickly, and did their job well. In combat it is important for the different branches of service to work together as much as possible. This ensures a more favorable outcome most times for everyone involved. I made sure I told their spotter to thank these pilots for their much-needed assistance that day.

Chapter 7:
Aftermath

"Only the dead have seen the end of war."
Plato

    We flew into that area as an understrength company. We flew out with even fewer men capable of fighting. Eight brave, young men gave their all. A ninth died ten days later in the hospital. The after-action report lists eighteen wounded. I believe this number to be incorrect. There were many survivors who we called "walking wounded." These troopers needed minor medical attention by our medics or by personnel at a firebase. They continued to serve with us in the jungle, so the number wounded must have been at least double the number in the report. However, our survival was a miracle considering the larger number of foes we faced that day.

    I don't remember where we relocated, but we had to stand down for several days to get replacements. Our effectiveness as a company unit was greatly strained from this battle. The mortar platoon was in bad shape and had to be rebuilt with new guys. The third platoon was also short on guys and needed replacements. The other two platoons fared much better, but could use additional people. I don't remember the recon platoon being with us during this battle. The action report does show them in a night position on October 23rd, where they received fire from RPGs and an unknown amount of small arms fire. They returned fire and ended the firefight with help from gunships.

We would lose ten more guys before my tour ended in June 1970. Dozens more would be wounded by that time. When the United States pulled out its combat forces in 1973, over 58,000 young men had given their lives for a war the American politicians would not allow us to win. Another 313,616 Americans came home with wounds from this war. Just about all of us combat grunts came back with invisible wounds; wounds of the heart and mind that would show up as Post Traumatic Stress. I believe combat is the most stressful thing a person can experience in life. We who have been in the trenches have seen horrible things that no one should have to see. We have done things that a person should not have to do. But in war, this cannot escape the infantry experience. This happens on a frequent basis. I've seen several guys trained just as we were, but they could not handle the horrors of combat. I also believe that there is a breaking point for all of us if subjected to enough hostile fire, bloodshed, and death. However, I did not see this with any of our seasoned veterans during my tour.

The fighting in August, September, and October helped me realize that there is nothing glorious about war as portrayed by Hollywood in the past. War, anyway you wish to describe it, is nothing but hell on earth. I don't know anyone who hates war more than those of us who have fought in one, unless it's the families of those who have given their lives in one. In spite of my hatred for war, I do believe that there are some good reasons to go to war as a last resort. Our nation's security, freedoms, and wellbeing, as well as that of our allies, are always at risk by our enemies, so protecting these can bring war to the front.

After our stand down, the company returned to the jungle with a lot of new guys. This would take time to bond again as a fighting unit. The mortar platoon would need to bond quickly to provide the best support for us when we needed them. We didn't need to get into a serious fight until these new guys could get some experience. On the 26th, we were in our night location when a trip flare activated, and two individuals were sighted. We blew claymores with no resulting hostile fire. First light revealed one NVA killed, but the other bad guy escaped. None of us were hurt.

On the 30th of October, the 2nd Brigade operation called Toan Thang III that began on August 1st, came to an end. Joining us during this trying time were other line companies assigned to the 1st Cav as well as engineers, signal units, artillery, aviation, and armored cav. We were opposed by a number of enemy units. They included the 5th VC Division and local force units, as well as the 86th rear service group. NVA regiments involved were 95A, 174th, and the 275th. During these three months, 451 NVA and 16 VC lost their lives to the brave fighting of the 1st Cav units. There is no figure for the number of enemy wounded, but it was significant because of the numerous blood trails. Six of the enemy were captured and became POWs. All of this action happened during the monsoon season, with 77 days of precipitation.

On November 1st, the 5/7 continued its operations around the big base called Buttons. Our company was operating near a river, which may have been the Song Be. Our mission called for us to cross this stream of water and patrol the other side. Someone volunteered to swim across and tie a rope along the bank. This would allow us to use our air mattresses to carry our rucksacks and weapons across without getting them wet. The guys who could not swim were also able to hold onto the rope. We all managed to cross safely and did not receive hostile fire. However, we had not gone very far on the other side when we ran into a small bunker complex. We began getting fire from one lone AK-47. As we returned fire, we also threw two concussion grenades into a bunker containing an unknown number of individuals. We never saw the guy firing the AK-47; he was not in a bunker, and he ceased firing shortly after we engaged him with our fire. He fled the area and did not leave a blood trail. We cautiously checked each bunker, finding two dead individuals in the one attacked with grenades. They appeared to be an elderly couple who must have been VC sympathizers because they should never have been in the jungle if their intentions were peaceful. The next day, we caught an individual on a trail without a weapon. We convinced him, very persuasively with weapons, to turn himself in to us. He could have been the bad guy who fired at us the day before.

November 4th, FSB Buttons received a heavy mortar and ground attack in the early morning hours. This was the two-hour attack I mentioned from our discovery of the firebase mockup of Buttons on August 26th. Enemy losses were substantial and a large quantity of weapons was captured.

FSB Buttons

    Starting on November 7th, the battalion became involved securing convoys traveling between Song Be and Phuoc Vinh. I only remember doing this several times working the road, partnering with an armored Cav unit. The after-action report does not record it, but I remember the convoy being ambushed once with minor injuries to transportation personnel. We did not have to get involved with the armored Cav's tremendous fire power. The Air Force also came to the rescue dropping heavy ordinance on the bad guys along the road. It was nice being able to watch the guys with greater firepower take care of the enemy without our assistance.

    The rest of the month was relatively peaceful. We were still working the jungle around FSB Buttons, but using a smaller base named Mary. It was located beside a major north to south highway. This road was nothing like our main highways in the states. It was just a dirt road and became much harder to travel on during the monsoon season. I am reminded of several things concerning this firebase. While we were providing security inside Mary early one morning, a South Vietnamese driving a box truck on this road ran over a mine. The explosion blew the entire rear housing and tires off the truck. The driver was not hurt and the cargo was a pleasant surprise to us. Inside were a number of blocks of ice that could not get to their destination. In the hot environment of Vietnam, ice was like having gold. We did our best to keep it from melting too soon.

The other thing I remember about firebase Mary is from my earlier days in my tour. I don't recall the time frame, but we were again the company providing security for the base. The battalion headquarters was also located on this base then and wanted the company to position LPs (listening posts) a hundred yards or more from the base perimeter during the nights. This was to provide early detection if the enemy assaulted the base. I hated this detail. I looked at it as a suicide mission. If the enemy attacked in the LP's direction, the three-man detail could be exposed leading to a very bad night. If the LP tried to get back to the base during the attack, there was the possibility of friendly fire taking it out. My buddy Harold tried to talk the squad leader against sending me on the first one because I was one of only three in the squad who was married. I appreciated Harold's concern, but I told him I was no better than anyone else and I would do my duty, just as every other squad member. Still, just three guys alone and a great distance from the base, we never felt safe, and those missions resulted in very little sleep during the night.

FSB Mary

T.O.C. (Tactical Operations Center)

    On Thanksgiving Day we were making our way to a landing zone to enjoy a turkey meal. Before breaking out of the jungle, we engaged a large individual on the trail killing him with our initial fire. He did not resemble a Vietnamese and stood approximately six feet tall and weighed probably 180-200lbs. We suspected him to be Chinese. Most of the Vietnamese people were no taller than 5 feet, 5 inches and weighed no more than probably 100 pounds. Battalion wanted us to send his body in and we placed him on the returning log bird. We were told that he was Chinese and must have been an advisor to the VC or NVA. I'm sure that's the reason this action is not mentioned on the action report for that day. China claimed that they had no soldiers in South Vietnam and the United States did not want to give them a reason to send large numbers of soldiers to fight against us.

    November ended as a very good month for A Company. There had been several minor skirmishes involving our sister companies, but nothing bad, with very few injuries. Evidently, our enemy retreated into Cambodia to recover from the beating we gave him in the previous three months.

    December began much like November ended, with very little action. B Company had several small firefights and FSB Mary received twelve mortar rounds on the 13th with no casualties. An armored ARVN unit was ambushed by a large force, losing six soldiers and three injured. However, the South Vietnamese killed fifteen enemy in this attack.

On December 16th, the entire battalion began moving to Phuoc Vinh to pull "Palace Guard" located at Camp Gorvad. There was no palace; it was the location of the 1st Cavalry Division Headquarters at the time. Division artillery HQ was also there. This area was known as the "rocket and mortar" belt. I found out years later that Phuoc Vinh was also "ground zero" for the spraying of Agent Orange in III Corp. All the companies began patrolling around this big base and getting heavily exposed to this toxic chemical. A number of guys in my battalion have already died from Agent Orange related illnesses as I write this memoir. To this date, I have not had any issues with exposure to this chemical. I feel very fortunate to continue to be healthy. We didn't realize we would be fighting another enemy years after our service in Vietnam ended.

The year ended with very little action and that did not anger us at all. We were still searching for trails, still carrying heavy packs, but we weren't running into the bad guys. By this time, Capt. Gary was rotated into battalion early after the October 20th ambush and was replaced by Capt. George. This officer was another good leader and was respected by everyone. I was fortunate to serve several months as his battalion RTO.

One thing I distinctly remember about Capt. George was his firm orders that every member of the company would shave during our log day when extra water was available. His RTO in his first tour had caught shrapnel in his face and the hair from his beard was embedded in the wounds, causing infection to set in and linger for an extended period of time. I also remember that the CO placed a new, young medic behind me when patrolling in single file order. This medic was nineteen, from Detroit, and I don't believe he had ever had a weapon in his hands until joining the Army. He kept his rifle aimed at the lower part of my back and I knew one day he was going to shoot me with his negligence. So I watched him like a hawk, telling him numerous times to point his weapon in the air or toward the ground. This became serious when he carelessly fired his M-16 on three occasions and, thankfully, did not hurt anyone. The CO took his weapon and issued him a 45-caliber pistol with a holster. I wondered why it took three firings but I was relieved to be free of this additional danger.

I learned early in December that there was an open spot for an R&R (rest and relaxation) during Christmas. I jumped at the chance to be away from Vietnam on such a special holiday. I was halfway through my tour and I would get to be with my wife again after such a long time. I was not sure how she would react to me, considering what I'd been through. But I didn't need to worry, she was excited to see me and the six days and five nights we had together in Hawaii was one of the best times we've shared in our long marriage. On that last day, it was really tough saying goodbye to my loving wife, knowing my destination, and what may lie ahead in my final six months.

When I processed through Saigon for my R&R, the first person I saw was Mack Bustle, a Statesville native from basic training. He was also meeting his wife in Hawaii during the same time. Our wives flew together from Charlotte and became acquainted during the flight. Sheila and I rented a car and drove all over the island. We invited Mack and Gertrude to go with us many times, enjoying each other's company. I'm so glad we spent that time with them because I learned later that Mack had died in a jeep accident about a month and a half after returning to his 1st Cav artillery unit in Vietnam. He is one of over ten thousand accidental deaths from the war. His name is on the "wall" in Washington D.C. and he is buried in Statesville, N.C. in Oakwood Cemetery.

R & R with wife in Hawaii

Chapter 8:
A New Approach

I have a secret plan to end the war.
Richard Nixon
37th President of the United States

    Richard Nixon was inaugurated on January 20, 1969, inheriting Lyndon Johnson's undeclared war. He had promised to end the war and promised to do so with American honor. His plan included continuing diplomacy and a major program of Vietnamization, where our modern weapons and equipment would be provided to the South Vietnamese military. Training the South Vietnamese to fight and protect themselves had been a part of the US strategy since the early 60s, when American military advisors were deployed there. Nixon was very much aware that a majority of Americans wanted our military to be brought home. So, the importance of preparing the South Vietnamese to defend their country without our help became a top priority. Some of the Vietnamese units were very good and fought with skill and courage, but many did not measure up. This was mostly due to poor leadership from top to bottom. There was also a lot of corruption in the government and ranks of the military. History would prove that this did not work, because the North Vietnamese launched a large attack in the south in April of 1975 and completely destroyed the South's military. Today, all of Vietnam is under heavy communist rule with very few liberties for their people.

All of this action by the new administration did not concern us as 1970 began. We were still patrolling the rocket and mortar belt around Phuoc Vinh and occasionally conducting convoy security on the roads in the area. The action reports show very little contact with the enemy. Having returned from my R&R, this inactivity by the bad guys did not hurt my feelings at all. If they didn't bother me, I sure wasn't interested in ruining their day. My days now in Vietnam were a little less than the days already served and I had not been injured yet. There were even rumors that some of us would get to go home early, starting in the spring. The president had already brought some units back to the US in August and September 1969. The only ones I remember leaving early were those with a month or less on their tour. Mike, my former squad leader was one of them.

The biggest problems we were having in the battalion during this period were careless accidents causing guys to be seriously injured or killed. It all came to a climax on February 8th. Our company combat assaulted into a relatively sparse area on that morning to begin patrolling. As usual, artillery provided cover fire around the LZ. The dry season had begun, and an artillery round had started a fire in the brush near our perimeter. In the initial flight of the first guys to land, rucksacks are dropped, and a perimeter is established. This is the most dangerous time on a combat assault with only a small number of guys on the ground during the first flight. Each succeeding flight (usually 3 or more, depending on the number of helicopters available) does the same until all the company is on the LZ. Without realizing, the fire spread to engulf one of the packs dropped early in the flight. A trooper saw this and reached to pull the rucksack from the fire. As he did this, the pack exploded, cutting him in half. The explosion killed another near him as well. Two other troopers were wounded. What a tragedy and a careless loss of two young men. PFC James Britt started his tour on December 3rd, 1969 and was a North Carolina native from Lumberton. PFC Wayne Woodland's life ended exactly one month from the day he started his tour. I have often wondered what the pack contained to cause it to explode. C4 would not explode by fire, so a claymore containing this explosive could not have blown without a blasting cap or some other explosion. No ammo was heard so there was no cook-off that may have exploded the claymore. My only conclusion was that there must have been at least one hand grenade that the pin melted from the heat, thus releasing the handle, causing the grenade to explode.

The battalion commander wanted this corrected immediately. He issued orders to all company commanders to initiate a safety class within twenty-four hours to all under their commands. The training would include the handling of weapons and grenades as well as the setting up and the disarming of ambushes. Fire hazards in the extremely dry grass and jungle would also be emphasized and a special note that tracers could also start a fire. I don't remember this training, but I'm sure it happened because our CO had to report back to his boss upon completion of this training.

I don't remember any further accidents after this training. However, on March 13th, I was assigned to headquarters to begin duty as a radio operator in the tactical operations center (TOC). I would once again join my best buddy Harold and I know he was putting in a good word for me when the opportunity arose. I thought I might get reassigned after returning from my R&R, but Capt. George would not release me. He wanted his experienced people to remain in place until he had some time commanding the company. Prior to my new assignment, we did continue to make contact with the enemy. On February 16th, we engaged two individuals, one carrying an AK-47 and the other one had a mortar tube on his shoulder. We must have been a little rusty with our aim because we found only blood trails. On the 22nd, we discovered a booby trap (known today as an IED) across a road. An EOD team was called out to eliminate this problem. There were fourteen explosive devices connected to this trap. How fortunate we were to find it. Many of us could have be killed or wounded had it not been spotted. On February 26th, we engaged several individuals resulting in wounding 8 VC. Later, two more were spotted, but escaped when the point man's weapon malfunctioned.

March 6th had us patrolling in more open country and we spotted two individuals that we believed to be woodcutters. They greeted us with small arms fire. We returned fire, but again were unsuccessful in stopping their escape. Five days later, we spotted two individuals armed with AK-47s, digging in an old firebase. We engaged them with small arms and had negative results. We must have been losing our shooting skills. However, we did find a blood trail heading west. The next day, March 12th, we spotted a VC in a clearing and engaged, but S.Sgt. Raymond Teal lost his life to this

59

enemy. The grenade and SKS rifle that the VC carried was not worth the life of this brave trooper.

     Patrolling in this more open area may have been the time that I almost gave away our company's position. We always tried to move as quietly as possible, even talking in a low whisper or using hand signals. We were walking single file, one behind the other, spaced appropriately, when out of the corner of my eye, I saw something sliding down a tree thirty yards away. I flipped my selector switch on my M-16 to automatic and almost fired until I realized this figure was a monkey about the size of a small man. I was the only one who saw this creature. This animal never knew how close he came to not being able to climb any more trees.

Chapter 9:
New Assignment

*The soldier above all other people prays for peace,
for he must suffer and bear the deepest wounds and scars of war.*
-General Douglas MacArthur
Southwest Pacific Commander, WWII

      Having been in a fairly active combat environment for nine months with death as a constant threat, my new job at headquarters appeared to be more peaceful and much safer. I would spend the remaining three months of my tour on a firebase working eight-hour shifts on the battalion radio. I would be able to see the bigger picture of the planning and implementing of our company's missions by the battalion commander and his staff. I would also be communicating with all our units in the jungle as they patrolled and made contact with the enemy. I continued to think of my buddies still facing combat and feared for the fights yet to come.
      Our battalion was still located in Phuoc Vinh with all companies patrolling the area. As I settled into my new job, I once again thought I had forfeited my chance at this promotion. Battalion always assigned two guys to monitor the radio at all times. The only exception was a trip to the latrine or to secure food while on duty. My partner left for one of those missions, leaving me as the lone monitor.

He had been gone just a minute or two when someone called on the landline telephone, which we also monitored. During this conversation the battalion commander was returning to headquarters in his helicopter and was calling in on the radio. I did not hear him calling and he was a commander who expected someone to answer him on his first call. By the time I finished the landline call he was very irate. He asked to speak with his XO, who was second in command. I quickly got the major's attention to talk to the commander. This CO wanted to know why I had not answered his call and told his XO to find someone else to do this job if I could not handle it. The XO did not realize what had happened, so he questioned me when the commander ended his call. I explained what happened and he evidently thought I needed a second chance, so I kept my job. For a few harried minutes, I thought I would be going back to the jungle the next day.

Phuoc Vinh was a big base, similar to LZ Buttons, with amenities available to us. I had a bed to sleep in located in a barracks built for that purpose. I could take a bath every day and eat hot meals in a mess hall. Almost like home! I was just beginning to enjoy all of this when an event happened that brought me back to reality. There was either an NCO club or an Officer's club next to my barracks; I cannot remember which. At this time in the war "fragging" had become a way of punishing bad leaders. A grenade would be used by a disgruntled GI to kill or injure a leader to send a message about his poor leadership or overly aggressive style. I never condoned this action at all. This was murder if the victim died. I had only been in my job a few days when someone threw a grenade into this club, just as I got in the bed. Much debris from this explosion splattered the side of the barracks where I was trying to sleep. I was so mad that I could have taken care of the guy who did this if I could have caught him. Here I was, a few days out of the jungle with some degree of normal living and this guy not only wanted to kill someone, but endangered those of us whom he did not know. I've read where leaders have been purposely killed or injured by friendly fire for the same reasons but I did not see this during my tour.

Our headquarters staff was actually located inside the division artillery compound, so it had a security fence around it. This allowed the MPs to immediately close the gates, keeping anyone from entering or leaving. Everyone within the compound was required to line up at the MP post to try to capture the "fragger". Within twenty minutes, he was found and taken into custody. I have no idea what happened to him but I'm sure he served time in jail before he was sent home and probably given a dishonorable discharge. Thankfully, I don't remember his stupid action hurting anyone.

    I was really beginning to get accustomed to the 8-hour duty and the rest of the day free to sleep, read, etc. But this fairly safe environment would come to an end on April 1, 1970. This is the day that our battalion would leave Phuoc Vinh and relieve 2nd battalion, 8th Cav at FSB Illingworth in Tay Ninh province. We were again moved to the "boonies". This firebase was named for Cpl. John James Illingworth, who was in A Company of this battalion and lost his life just the month before near Tay Ninh City. We were just a few short miles from the Cambodian border and positioned in direct routes that the NVA used to attack villages from the border all the way to Saigon in the south.

    At 2:18 AM on that day, the first of 300 NVA mortars, rockets, and recoilless rifle rounds began exploding inside Illingworth's perimeter in a 20-minute barrage. The artillery fire direction centers were taken out almost immediately. Soon thereafter, some 400 NVA and Viet Cong soldiers charged the perimeter in a full-frontal attack. The battle was fierce, and some artillery men joined the infantry at the point of attack to keep from being overrun. Hand-to-hand fighting was prevalent in areas of the perimeter and the situation was getting critical. Then, at 3:18 AM, a bunker containing about 190 rounds of 8-inch artillery shells exploded with a tremendous blast, knocking most off their feet and deafening many. There was sporadic fighting after this, but the blast broke the back of the attack and the enemy had faded away by 5:00 AM, leaving 88 bodies behind. A total of 25 GIs were killed and 54 wounded. Spec. 4 Peter Lemon was awarded the Medal of Honor for his actions that morning, with two Distinguished Service Crosses awarded posthumously to his E Company buddies. Additionally, 12 Silver Stars were awarded; nine posthumously.

    We flew into Illingworth by helicopter about mid-morning with our battalion companies providing mop-up operations so the ambushed battalion could prepare to leave and get a deserved stand-down to recover. With approximately two and a half months to serve in my tour, dangerous combat became a dreaded reality again. The firebase showed the true effects of two forces trying to destroy each other. The destruction was almost total across the base. The faces of the survivors revealed the horror and anguish of the battle that nearly wiped them out. We were told that some of the NVA dead had wires around their legs so they could be dragged away from battle, preventing us from getting a proper number of enemy KIAs. That explained the times we believed we killed more enemy than we found after the fight. The blood trails were evidence of this. I had heard of this during my tour, but had never seen the wires attached, so I ventured to the edge of the woods and saw regular NVA soldiers in dark green uniforms; some with the wires around their legs.

FSB Illingworth destruction. April 1, 1970

FSB Illingworth

So, this was the environment where we re-deployed. We were very close to the Cambodian border, and I admit that I was nervous and afraid for our security. I knew that a battle here could very well happen again, but this time it would be the 5/7 involved and I didn't care to fight any more. By this time in my tour, I had almost convinced myself that I was going to get home without being wounded.

Evidently, the battalion commander realized the effects this destroyed base could have on our morale, so we did very little to restore the base. A few days later we moved farther down the valley and established a new one named FSB Wood. This would be my new home for a time, but I did not know that we would move again in a month. We received a change of command during our stay here with Lt. Col. Maury taking over. He was a very capable leader, and I don't know anyone who did not like him. He continued his career in the Army after serving in Vietnam and retired as a Major General. I have been fortunate to renew my friendship with him in recent years as he became our 5/7 association president, serving in that position for 10 years. LTC. Maury had been very aware of the battle at Illingworth when he took command and immediately made plans to effectively counter any attacks that the NVA might have for us. The companies patrolling the area were advised to be very cautious to avoid enemy ambushes. The artillery was tasked with firing into the wood line at various times during the night. In the event of an attack, the S2, Capt. Troy, and I would make our way to another location on the firebase and provide radio communication if the TOC was taken out of commission.

As our companies began patrolling around FSB Wood, enemy activity appeared to be light. But this would change very quickly. D Company found a battalion size training center that contained a mock-up of a firebase. Sightings and other signs by one of our aviation support units indicated the enemy was moving back into the area. By April 14th, some contact was beginning with small size enemy units and ten days later, the NVA was spotted trying to recon the base. This activity continued for the remaining days of April and by the 3rd of May, the enemy was ready to strike again, just as they did against FSB Illingworth. The NVA started placing their units in the woods to the north of our firebase after dark on the 3rd and were still forming up at approximately 10:20 when the artillery began firing air burst rounds into the treetops. This caused the enemy to begin their assault before they were ready. The action report records 10-15 mortar rounds landing inside the base, but I remember more than that. I had just gone to bed when one of those mortars landed out in front of my sandbagged culvert. Everybody on the perimeter began firing their weapons with additional help from the artillery and a couple of tanks assigned to us for defensive purposes. Our aviation support spotted two 51 caliber anti-aircraft guns and I believe they were taken out. The report of this attack does not indicate the destruction of these guns. Capt. Troy and I immediately went to our designated location, where I monitored the radio during the attack. The rapid response from the firebase made a big difference in the outcome. Sporadic fire continued until midnight, but after that beating, the NVA evidently had enough. They left behind over 200 KIAs and 3 POWs; we had 11 wounded and one artillery crewman killed at the beginning of the attack. In this one, we took the enemy to the cleaners and also helped to avenge the attack at Illingworth. After daybreak, I saw all of the war material the recon units brought in and was very thankful to survive another battle without a scratch. I also watched as Capt. Troy questioned the enemy POWs to get information from them. One of the captured was an NVA battalion commander who stated that two battalions attacked us that night.

  To our great surprise, we received orders to leave FSB Wood this same day for a new area of operations. It would be a dangerous mission no one expected.

Chapter 10:
Cambodian Incursion

Our neutrality has been imposed on us by necessity.
-King Norodom Sihanouk

Cambodia was a country in the 1960s about the size of Missouri with a population of better than four million people, consisting of mostly peasant farmers. Its border extended almost two-thirds of the length of South Vietnam which made it ideal to use for the trail system connecting it to Laos in the North. During the Cold War years of the 1950s and early 1960s, the United States sent millions of dollars into Cambodia to build its economy and strengthen its Armed Forces. Sihanouk feared for his country's survival with the expansionary policies of the Russians and Chinese. He reached out to other nations to help defend his country if it became necessary. The United States was not eager to be the protector of Cambodia. We were providing resources at that time to South Vietnam trying to prevent communist expansion from North Vietnam and its allies, Russia and China. So, the king tried to appease everybody by being neutral. However, this did not last very long, as the North Vietnamese and Viet Cong used the trail system in his country to transport men and material in their war against the South. They also established rest areas and built storage facilities near these trails. Eventually Sihanouk looked the other way, since the communists allowed him to stay in power and by early 1965, he aligned himself with them.

Since March of 1969, President Nixon had authorized the Air Force to bomb these trails and sanctuaries in Cambodia. These missions were to remain secret to the public and the news media. By May 1, 1970, the President was ready to do more to help the South Vietnamese take military control of their country when we finally pulled out. He believed destroying these areas and the enemy who used them would contribute much to the success of South Vietnam's future. On April 30, 1970, President Nixon announced to a television audience that he would be sending US military units into Cambodia to attack these enemy sanctuaries and destroy the headquarters for the entire Communist military operation in South Vietnam. This was the mission; it would not be an easy one. The North Vietnamese would be expected to protect their military assets at all costs. The plans had been made. It was time for action.

One More Time

My first thought after hearing that we would invade Cambodia (although it was called an incursion) was that combat strength would be extremely important in this mission. I suspected that I could be reassigned to my former company with my experience as a grunt. I was promoted to sergeant on May 3rd and could easily have been assigned a squad to lead. Being near the end of my tour, I was not eager to get back in the fight. I was also getting worried that I would be wounded in this large scale mission with a short time left to serve. But like any good soldier, I would have gone back to the jungle if ordered. Regardless of my remaining duty, I prayed that my buddies in the bush would survive this dangerous mission.

We left FSB Wood at 12:15 PM by helicopter after turning the base over to the 25th Infantry Division and flew to Thiew Ngon for airstrip transport to a battalion location prior to pushing into Cambodia. On May 6th, the Battalion moved across the border and established FSB Brown to begin operations. The 1st Cav was the largest American force committing 7,401 troopers in this operation. We were joined by the 11th Armored Cav in the fishhook area. The 4th, 9th and 25th infantry divisions would also take part, some invading the dog's head area farther south. Thirty thousand American troops and forty-eight thousand ARVN (South Vietnamese Army) soldiers were involved before the mission ended on June 30th.

The first few days resulted in very little contact with the enemy, so we moved farther inland and to the northeast. Just a few days after leaving FSB Brown, this base was attacked by an NVA unit for two hours and nearly overrun. With our move, trouble started immediately. On May 9th, A Company assaulted a hillside and was quickly surrounded and fighting for their lives. They received support from gunships and artillery while fighting bravely for three hours before the NVA decided they had enough. Sadly, Sgt. Chester Hall, who I knew, lost his life and seven more troopers were wounded. C and D Companies were inserted into the vicinity of the battle, where a new firebase was built several days later, called FSB Neal. This would be my home for the remainder of my tour. D Company had the task of constructing this new base while the other companies conducted ground operations in the area. I even had the opportunity to fill sandbags when not on duty with the radio. They would do much in protecting me while in my sleeping quarters.

C Company found a cache on May 14th, containing over one ton of rice. Several weapons were also found at this site. On May 15th, A and C Companies were ordered to move farther south to find another suspected cache. The next day, A Company had an automatic ambush detonate, resulting in two NVA KIAs. They continued to push south and by May 17th, the contact was extremely heavy involving not only A and C Companies, but also B Company. There were six separate firefights that day with two troopers giving their all and twenty-five others wounded. The next day, four more contacts were made with A Company capturing an NVA soldier. May 19th became the big day that Battalion was expecting from the beginning. The fighting had been heavy and it was suspected that the enemy was protecting something very important that they didn't want to lose. B Company found a bunker complex with documents, medical supplies, and tons of rice. A Company was nearing its objective when the 1st platoon came under heavy fire from grenades, RPGs, and small arms. Soon the company was taking fire from the flanks as well. The mortar platoon sprang into action and quickly expanded its ammo. The lead platoon at the very point of contact was running out of ammunition. Mortar platoon leader Jack realized this and asked for volunteers to help him rush ammo to the point platoon. He also took command with the acting platoon leader wounded. Without Lt. Jack's actions, the survivors in that platoon remarked that they would not have survived. Lt. Jack and Sgt. Tom, the acting platoon leader, both received Silver Stars for their bravery that day. The machine gunner, PFC Larry Rigney, was also awarded a Silver Star posthumously. Corporal Lewis Earl Cox gave his life in this six hour battle that day as well.

The next day, A Company reached their objective, but not without casualties. Corporals Jackie Ford and James Hazard lost their lives trying to capture an important military cache. It was the largest cache of medical supplies found in Cambodia. In the days that followed, A Company discovered what appeared to be a dispensary complex, with bunkers containing several operating rooms. A continued search netted 627 cases of medical supplies. The enemy was willing to fight for their much needed military material. It cost us dearly in lives lost and many wounded. Was the mission worth it? I cannot answer except to say that the facts are clear that the enemy could not launch a major attack in III Corp for a long time after this incursion ended.

Treasure Chest

A Company would lose one more trooper, Corporal Keith Held, before the mission ended. They continued to search the area in the vicinity of the medical bunker and found a large cache of rice, over 60 tons. This rice was given to a large number of Montagnards who came to FSB Neal after they were forced out of their village by the NVA. These people were a different race from the Vietnamese and usually lived very primitively in mountainous regions. They were good fighters helping us in the war but there was no love between these two peoples. The Battalion helped to resettle these mountain people into a new village. After the war, our nation helped many of them immigrate to our country.

B Company was successful in finding the prize for the entire mission. On May 22nd, after five continuous days of contact, they came under intense small arms fire that lasted for an hour. The enemy was protecting 50 storage bunkers containing enormous quantities of weapons, ammunition, and other equipment vital to their war effort. This became one of the largest caches found in the incursion. It was named "Shakey's Hill" by B Company troopers in memory of PFC Chris Keffalos, who died from the small arms fire at the beginning of the assault.

A CBS camera crew was with B Company during this assault and interviewed some of the troopers and filmed some of the action. In 2004, the cameraman shooting the video of B Company visited our Battalion reunion. Norman Lloyd wanted to make a documentary of our participation in the incursion featuring B Company, using the video from 1970. He also interviewed some of the same guys from the battle thirty-four years earlier. *Commitment and Sacrifice* became available at our reunion in 2006 and is a good account of what actually happened during this Cambodian mission.

During the 53 days that the Battalion conducted operations inside Cambodia, it was responsible for 52 enemy KIAs and 2 prisoners, the capture of 839 individual weapons, 220 crew served weapons, and over 1.3 million rounds of ammunition. The discovery and evacuation of over 305 tons of rice and 1,213 cases of medical supplies were stocked-piled back in South Vietnam. Also captured were 16 vehicles and over 10 tons of repair parts. All of these military supplies were enough to equip five NVA infantry battalions to launch numerous attacks against us. The tons of rice and other food stuffs found was enough to feed 10 NVA infantry companies full rations for a year.

The two-month Cambodian operation resulted in 354 American deaths among all units involved and 1,689 wounded with 13 missing. The South Vietnamese deaths totaled 866 with 3,724 wounded. The communist enemy deaths were estimated at over 12,000.

Home Sweet Home

The Cambodian incursion was very successful in taking a lot of war making material away from the enemy, but no one was able to locate the headquarters that executed North Vietnam's war at the local level. I felt very fortunate to be on a firebase out of the line of fire the last month and a half of my tour. However, I was directly involved in the communications of this mission as I took my turn on the radio talking with the various units doing the fighting. It was during those times that I responded to the actions taking place and listened to the battalion commander and his staff co-ordinate the support needed by those units in battle. I always had concern for the guys in the fight, especially those from my former company. I still knew a lot of them and felt nothing but sorrow knowing exactly what they were going through.

Radio duty during Cambodian incursion

I left my job in the TOC on or about the 10th or 12th of June to fly back across the border to begin processing to return home. I was ready and anxious to see home and family again. I still had six months of active duty to serve in Uncle Sam's Army but would receive some leave before reporting to my next duty station.

My date of return to "the world" as we called it, was June 22nd. I landed by helicopter on our big base Buttons from Cambodia and began processing. With my only duty of obtaining the paperwork to leave South Vietnam, I had extra time and days to unwind before my departure.

During the processing I found that I was being awarded several medals that caught me by surprise. I knew that the Vietnam Service and Vietnam Campaign medals were givens. I did not expect a Bronze Star, a Commendation Medal and an Air Medal. None of these were actually presented to me in any formal setting. When I had taken my R&R back in December, I was told that I had been awarded a CIB. That was the only award that I wore on my uniform to Hawaii. I learned later that all of us in the battalion were awarded the Army Valorous Unit Citation as well as the RVN Gallantry Cross Unit Citation and the RVN Civic Action Honor Medal Unit Citation. The army valor citation was awarded for our actions in the Cambodian mission.

I believe I flew from Buttons to Bien Hoa on the 20th of June to do the final clearing from Vietnam. I spent the night there and was lucky to get a flight out the next morning. The commercial airliner was full of military personnel ending their tours. New guys just beginning their duty in Vietnam had arrived a short time earlier on this same plane. I knew how they must have felt starting their tours and I did feel some sorrow for them, even knowing my replacement could have been on this plane. After the plane was refueled, and clearance given for takeoff, our flight began with very little talking, even with the friendly American flight attendants. After clearing the coastline, there was a tremendous "hoorah" and the talking and laughing began. All of us had made it and these young stewardesses treated us like royalty on our trip back to the states.

What Now?

I now know why men who have been to war yearn to reunite. Not to tell stories or look at old pictures. Not to laugh or weep. Comrades gather because they long to be with men who once acted at their best; men who suffered and sacrificed, who were stripped of their humanity. I did not pick these men. They were delivered by fate and the military. But I know them in a way I know no other man. I have never given anyone such trust. They were willing to guard something more precious than my life. They would have carried my reputation, the memory of me. It was part of the bargain we all made, the reason we were so willing to die for one another. As long as I have memory, I will think of them all, every day. I am sure that when I leave this world, my last thought will be of my family and my comrades…such good men.

Author Unknown

Joe Foss, a WWII fighter ace and recipient of the Medal of Honor must have had the same thought when he said, "Those of us who have lived have to represent those who didn't make it." I will never forget those 19 troopers in A Company who gave the ultimate sacrifice during my tour with them. From this time in combat and many days since, I've wondered why I survived and they didn't. Like many war veterans, I have some guilt associated with that fact. But I have concluded that I made it because of four things. The troopers with whom I served were truly brothers-in-arms. They were keeping me alive with their bravery. My wife, family, and church were so supportive by writing and by praying for my safety and wellbeing. Additionally, my faith in a loving God contributed much in my ability to accept the things happening around me. Finally, I believe God had more for me to do in serving him, so he has given me more time on this earth.

  My career after the military has been about serving people. I have done this with my church and my years with the postal service. I have since found this calling to be with military veterans. I have been heavily involved with Welcome Home Veterans at Richard's Coffee Shop in Mooresville, N.C. for the last eleven years. It was established by a helicopter gunship pilot by the name of Richard Warren, who served in Vietnam during the same time of my tour. Welcome Home Veterans is a non-profit organization whose main purpose is helping veterans. After Richard's death in 2009, we've continued to keep his vision alive by assisting veterans in any way we can. I've looked at my participation as a ministry, trying to honor and represent those who gave their lives on my behalf. I don't believe that's asking too much.

Regimental Crest, ¼ of 1st infantry division

PART II
Chapter 1:
Cold War Service

I still had six months active duty in the Army when I came home in the summer of 1970. My orders allowed me 30 days leave before reporting to the 1st Infantry Division (The Big Red One) stationed at Fort Riley, Kansas. What a wonderful time with my wife, family, and friends after so long being away from them all! I enjoyed every minute, but it was strange trying to adjust again to a more peaceful time without hearing explosions, rifle and machine gun fire, and the other sounds of combat.

For this remaining duty, Sheila would be allowed to be with me if I could find a place to live. So we rented a U-Haul to carry our essentials and pulled it with our brand new Dodge Charger to Kansas. The living quarters on post were reserved for higher ranking NCOs, so we would have to live off post. Trying to find such a place became a chore. We tried to find a furnished apartment, but to no avail. Then we searched for one unfurnished and was about to give up when one became available in Junction City. It was an old wooden barracks from the post that the landlord had bought and made into four different apartments. We had to get the Army to ship some of our furniture there for my final months of service. It would have been cheaper for the military if they had released me when I returned from

Vietnam because they covered the expense of shipping our furniture home as well.

Fort Riley! How ironic! I would be traveling the very ground that George Custer and his 7th Cavalry traveled almost one hundred years before. I checked in with my orders on July 30th to the 1st Squadron, 4th Cavalry. This was an armored unit with tanks and other track vehicles. I wondered why I, an infantryman, was assigned to armor. But at least I would get to ride most of the time and would not have to carry a heavy pack on my back.

The 1st Squadron, 4th Cav was known as "Quarterhorse" and had distinguished itself in over one hundred and twenty years of military service to our country. It was involved in the Indian wars, the Civil War, Philippine insurrection, World War II, and Vietnam. In fact, the unit had just returned from Vietnam in February prior to my reporting in July. Once again, I became a member of a very highly regarded military unit. "Quarterhorse" was also a part of the "Big Red One," an Army division well known for its history and legacy dating back to WWI. It was organized on June 8, 1917 and sailed to France entering combat in October. One of their best known battles was in the Meuse-Argonne Forrest near the end of the war.

I checked in with the first sergeant, who assigned me to a squad, telling me that I would
be the squad leader. There were two sergeants already assigned to this squad so I felt that one of them should be the leader. They were also Vietnam veterans and had been at the post a couple of weeks before me. I told the first sergeant that I would rather not be the squad leader, but he told me in no uncertain terms that I was the leader even though I didn't want the responsibility. He must have seen something in me that I thought he should have seen in the other two sergeants. They were very competent, and I believe would have done just as well, if not better, than I did. I did appoint them as my fire-team leaders.

Our mission as a division was much different from our training for Vietnam. We were responsible for preventing Russia from invading Germany. If this ever became reality, the combat would resemble that from WWII. So, during the summer, we spent several weeks at different times and some weekends practicing combat for this type of war. Our tank crews spent some of this time re-qualifying to be the best at hitting targets. The tanks were the up-to-date Sheridans, entering service in 1969 in Vietnam. They were a light tank with a 152 MM cannon that could also fire Shillelagh missiles. They served us well until they were taken out of service in 1996.

I was getting settled into my responsibilities and accustomed to going home every day after duty when we received word that we would be participating in a NATO exercise in Germany during the month of October. It would be called "Reforger II." The Air Force would fly us to Germany in C-141s to play war against the German Army and the US military stationed there. This would give the Army a good idea how well our training had prepared us for an attack from Russia.

We flew to Stuttgart and assembled in a forest where tanks and other track vehicles had been stationed there for us. We left our own equipment at Fort Riley. I believe we stayed at this location two nights and left late in the afternoon to load these vehicles on rail cars for a night trip close to the Czechoslovakian border. This is where we played war for a week. I remember during this week that we were eating c-rations at every meal. I was talking by radio to a squad leader of a tank crew about wanting a hamburger to eat. He told me to come to his location. I had my driver of our APC to drive us to his spot and found his tank in the bushes across from a nice German restaurant. He said we could purchase something better to eat at this restaurant. We were still in a war games situation and would have been in trouble if caught. But we escaped trouble and had a good supper. However, it was not a hamburger. I remember that I had to take my squad on a recon mission during this week, looking for our war games enemy or any suspicious thing that might lead to the Russians spying on us as we played war. I don't remember seeing anything unusual.

At the end of our war games, we stood down at Grafenwoehr, an old WWII German base. We slept in WWII German cinder block barracks while there and had the opportunity to take a tour into Nuremberg. This was the place where Hitler held those big Nazi rallies at Zeppelin field, with the large concrete podium that he stood on to give speeches. The old newsreels from WWII show thousands standing in formation for hours as he gave his speeches. Nuremberg was also the town the allies picked to prosecute Nazi war criminals after the war ended because of its importance as a Nazi stronghold. Most of the town was destroyed during the war, but by 1970 it had been rebuilt as a modern city. It was well worth the time to visit this town with such a historic past even before Hitler came to power. The entire month in Germany was a special treat. Knowing that my heritage on both sides of my family was German gave me an opportunity to see the country of my lineage. My dad, having fought there, may have even clashed with relatives. I certainly hope none of them were Nazis, but that could be a possibility. The people we met were very friendly and seemed to be pleased that we were in their country.

At the end of October, the Air Force flew us back to Fort Riley where we resumed more training to correct any mistakes made in our war games. The day I landed, I called Sheila, who had gone home to be with her mother during my time in Germany. My parents were planning to visit us when I returned and wanted Sheila to travel with them so she wouldn't be alone on the trip back to Kansas. But she wouldn't wait and left the day I returned. My parents left a day later and we all had a great time during their visit. We gave them a tour of Fort Riley and the surrounding Kansas countryside.

Not long after returning from Germany, Sheila suspected she was pregnant. She scheduled an appointment with a doctor and he assured her that she was in the early weeks of a pregnancy. We did not tell our parents because we knew they would be concerned with us so far away. So, we waited until I was discharged in January, 1971. By that time, she could not hide her pregnancy so the parents were very excited to welcome a new baby boy into the family. Richard was born June 18, 1971. A younger brother, Phillip, would follow three years later on August 1st. They have families of their own now and have given Sheila and me four wonderful grandchildren.

By now, my time in the Army and at Fort Riley was getting short but I still had to report for duty during the week and occasionally on weekends. Sometimes it involved going back to base after duty hours. One night at about 9:00 PM, my platoon sergeant called and informed me to report back to the barracks for further orders. He would not tell me the reason over the phone. Reporting to him, I was tasked with taking a squad to our motor pool to check all our vehicles, making sure everything was in perfect order. I knew they would be ok, so I asked the reason for this because I saw others in the barracks cleaning weapons. He said that the battalion commander would receive an award if his battalion placed first in an inspection. I was getting a short-timers attitude by this time and did not appreciate having to return at night for duty just so the commander might get an award. For the first few weeks at Fort Riley, I did not have a phone, so there was no way for headquarters to reach me after duty. But this ended when I went in one morning after an IG inspection had taken place during the night. All the guys had been up most of the night, so I missed this big one but I had to give them my phone number at that time.

Another after-duty job involved guarding post facilities. I had done this once during my initial training when I entered the Army. Now, as a sergeant, I would not have to physically guard anything but was picked to be the NCO in charge of the guys who were detailed for this duty. I would have to inspect each guard to be sure they were neat and clean and their uniform was the same. If they were not at their best, they were removed from this duty and faced disciplinary punishment. Guard duty was important to the military and everyone involved had to look sharp and be on their best behavior. The officer of the guard checked us as well before the duty began. I usually didn't get much sleep during this duty because I had to make sure the guards were reporting to their stations at the correct times during the night. The officer and I would also check the guards on duty to be sure they were properly guarding as their orders directed.

CQ duty was also an off-duty assignment that rotated between us NCOs. This stood for charge-of-quarters, which meant I would be in the company office answering any phone calls, checking security inside and outside the building during the night, and anything else that happened within my responsibility. There would also be an officer who I would report to if I needed assistance in any way. This was another duty that did not allow much sleep. I used my APC driver as my runner for the night who usually told me to take a nap. But I was afraid he would fall asleep as well and I knew that I would be the one in trouble if caught napping.

My last CQ duty was scheduled for Thursday before being discharged the following Monday. I had to turn in equipment and do other processing on Friday morning. This meant that my last chance at sleep was Wednesday night. I would be performing my responsibilities for over thirty hours without the benefit of sleep. The first sergeant who assigned me originally had volunteered for a second tour in Vietnam and was no longer in the company. He had a policy that allowed a soldier with thirty days left in the Army to be taken from the off-duty list. But the new first sergeant who replaced him did not have such a policy. I tried to explain to him my situation but he wouldn't listen. He told me I would do my duty as assigned. I finally got to bed at 2:00 PM on Friday afternoon. I felt like choking the first sergeant.

My platoon sergeant was more understanding and a great guy who had been in the army eighteen years. He had served in Germany several times and was married to a German woman. He had not gotten orders for Vietnam until a few months prior to my discharge. I thought this to be bad timing with his needing only two more years of service before he could retire. But he appeared to be ready and willing to do his part. He also encouraged me to re-enlist because he thought I was a leader that the army needed in its future. He believed I could be promoted to Staff Sergeant within a year if I chose to remain in the army. I appreciated his confidence in me, but I told him that I suspected a second tour in Vietnam would be in my future if I stayed in the army. I had survived without a scratch and my chances a second time would probably not be as good. I also reminded him that being in combat arms; the army could ship us out overnight to a hot spot in the world without much concern for family members. I understood this reality with combat arms but was unwilling to continue this life beyond my required duty. I believe the military does a much better job today making sure that family members are taken care of while their loved one is deployed out of the country.

Home Again-At Last

On Monday, January 26, 1971, I was free from active duty with the Army. I still had two years of active reserve and two years of inactive reserve time. Each enlisted person serving in the military had a total of six years with reserve time. However, with the war continuing and so many joining the reserves, I did not have any active reserve time at all. So, I was basically finished with my service on that cold Kansas morning. Sheila and I had to spend two more nights in Kansas so that the Army could pick up our furniture and get it back to North Carolina. They came the next morning and we spent that night with a veteran and his wife in the apartment next to us.

On our trip home, we stopped in Nashville for the night. Sometime during those hours, an ice storm hit the area. We started before daylight on the slick roads and hadn't gone very far when we turned completely around on the ice, heading the same direction we were going. My fear was hitting something, injuring Sheila, and losing our unborn baby. However, we were fortunate to escape a wreck and injury. The rest of our trip home was uneventful except for the pleasure of getting back to North Carolina and home.

After a short vacation, I went back to my job at Troutman Industries for two years. I was then employed part-time with the postal service and entered Rowan Technical Institute using my GI education benefits. I graduated with an associate degree in electronics engineering technology and continued working for the post office, retiring after thirty years.

Less than 1% of the American population ever serves in the military. The only exception was WWII. I am proud to be in that small number. I believe my service has made me a better person and a more responsible citizen of my community, state and nation. Under the same circumstances, I would serve again if that were possible. Without those willing to serve, our nation's freedoms would begin to vanish. What a great country we are fortunate to live in!

ACKNOWLEDGMENTS

This book would not be available to the public without the encouragement of fellow Vietnam veteran John Hedley. It was to be written only for family, but he convinced me that the American people need to know what the combat soldier experienced in a controversial war, one where the country's leadership gave up and the warriors who fought it lost the people's support. Thank you, John, for your inspiration.

My thanks also to a very special retired English teacher, Jean Brown, who made sure my sentences were correctly written with the proper punctuation. Very helpful in this endeavor has been David Parkins, whose guidance and assembling of the manuscript and pictures to present to the publisher has not been unnoticed. Cotton Ketchie, a well-known artist and photographer, was instrumental in getting the print used for the cover of this book to a size the publisher needed. I especially thank Joe Kline, a Vietnam veteran himself, who has allowed the use of his print, "Kicking the Hornets' Nest", as the cover for my book. Special thanks also to a young college student and friend, Mikayla Hord, who transcribed the manuscript from written to digital. Finally, a heartfelt thanks to Pete Donnelly and staff at A15 Publishing who took a chance on me and made this happen.

REVIEWS

The book, "Pop Smoke: The Memoir of a 1st Air Cavalry Division Infantry Grunt" by Sgt. Ralph Dagenhart is a great source for the story of what Vietnam was really like for an infantryman patrolling the jungles and rice paddies. Unlike many other books of this type, this fine work contains no political or anti-military content. Everything is related just as it happened. Reading this book is a great way to get into the grunt's head as he experiences all of the emotions of combat and can lead to a much better understanding of the war and its effect on those who fought it. I heartily recommend it for any veteran or student of the war.

John Hedley, LTC Infantry (Ret)
4th Infantry Division
Vietnam 1969-70

As a Vietnam war veteran, I can say that "War is hell on earth" and no one wins except those who live through it and come out without being too twisted to live a "normal" life and enjoy God, family, and friends. Ralph did just that.

Combat (and war in general) is sheer terror for a young soldier who starts out thinking he is "bullet proof" in his own mind-even though he can see his friends being killed or wounded all around him. Courage is fighting through the horror and coming out the other side physically intact but mentally deeply wounded.

Putting into words the fear, mental torture, hatred, and negative thoughts fighting to kill another human being come very hard, but Ralph Dagenhart has done a great job in describing the actual day to day experiences of this ugly deed.

Unless you have personally seen, lived through, and experienced these images of the atrocity that must happen in battle, your imagination cannot comprehend what killing up close can and will do to young men. The thoughts never go away. Losing friends and killing the "enemy" is with you to the end of your life. This book took courage to write – to "open that little box" in the very back of his mind. Ralph did it very well.

Larry S. Campbell
Chief Warrant Officer 2
Helicopter Pilot, 1st Air Cavalry Division
Vietnam 1967-68

Well done! It is faithful in telling the story of an infantry soldier in combat in a very tough environment to which it was frequently hard to find and confront the enemy before he could confront you. The courage of our troopers and their leaders, and, their commitment to their missions and to each other deserve to be hailed as among the best in our history. Your narrative adds to that legend. Congratulations!
MG Maurice O. Edmonds, USA (Retired)
Commander, 5th Battalion, 7th Cavalry
Vietnam, 1970

I found your memoir very trut to combat operations of which I participated. Although I am not a Vietnam veteran, your testimony explains very well the burden of an infantry soldier to close with and destroy the enemy which I witnessed so well in Panama and Iraq.
MG Chuck H. Swannack, Jr. USA (Retired)
Commander, 82d Airborne Division
Deputy Commanding General, 18th Airborne Corps

It is a fun read and highlights what life in the Army is like. A good diary of your service to our nation. Enjoyed it very much.
Lt Col John Beyerle, USAF (Retired)
Pilot, F4, C-130, B-52
Vietnam, 3 tours

EPILOGUE

From the very beginning of this memoir, I stated that my military experience changed me and has had a lasting effect on my life. Things I have seen and done that could be considered a negative and dark period in my life, have only been positive, in my opinion. In looking back, I believe my experience confirmed what I already knew or was taught. First, all of us can do more than we believe we can do. The teachers in school that I disliked the most were the ones who were the strictest and required the most homework and testing. They were trying to get the most out of me, proving that I had more to give. This is so true with the military and in everyday life. Second, most of us are not hermits. We are surrounded by people of diverse backgrounds. We must depend on each other for the relationships we have with them. I hope that this has been made very clear in this book how critical we grunts depended on each other. Obviously, these close relationships were formed in extreme circumstances, but this can also be true no matter what path our lives take us. I believe we've been placed on this earth for a reason and that is to help each other, to be there for others in good times and bad. Third, life and living is a creation of God. Every person is special and created in his image. To take human life or destroy it in some way is the ultimate desecration of mankind. War is a horrible way to solve problems. Fourth, we live in the best country in the world. Most of us did not choose to be born here. We have been so blessed as citizens of this country. We have freedoms here that people in other countries just dream about. I feel so much more patriotic and thankful now than before my military service. Finally, things that we thought were so important before, take a back seat to the critical ones today. We tend to worry or argue about insignificant things while lives could be much better if we solved the tough problems together.

May this book be an inspiration to you and your place in this world.
Ralph Dagenhart

ABOUT THE AUTHOR

Sergeant Ralph Dagenhart served a one-year tour in the Vietnam War with the historic 1st Cavalry Division (Air Mobile) as an infantry rifleman and Radio Telephone Operator (RTO). His last month and a half was in the Cambodian Incursion operation known as "Rock Crusher" where many tons of North Vietnamese military equipment was taken from the enemy. His combat decorations include the Combat Infantry Badge, Bronze Star, Air Medal, Army Commendation, and the Army Valorous Unit Citation.

REFERENCES

Operational Report of 2nd Brigade, 1st CAV Div (Air Mobile) for period ending 31 October, 1969/Declassified

Department of the Army
14th Military Detachment
1st Cavalry Division (Air Mobile)
7 March, 1970

Department of the Army
Headquarters, 5th Battalion, 7th Cavalry (Air Mobile)
Weekly After Action Reports
Vietnam, 1969-1970

Brutal Battles of Vietnam: America's Deadliest Days 1965-1972
VFW ISBN 978-0-9743643-4-6
Library of Congress Catalog Number 2017943415

Know Your Enemy: The Viet Cong
DoD GEN-20

Made in the USA
Coppell, TX
03 July 2024

34227490R00059